Inward Bound

Living Life from the Inside Out

Inward Bound

Living Life from the Inside Out

Alexander Everett

BookPartners, Inc.
Wilsonville, Oregon

BookPartners, Inc.
P.O. Box 922
Wilsonville, Oregon 97070

I dedicate this book to all my students, the men and women I've taken through the process of Inward Bound. *They have given back to me a spiritual satisfaction that is a reflection of their expanded consciousness.*

Table of Contents

Foreword

I met Alexander Everett in 1985 while he was presenting Inward Bound seminars in his home at Veneta, Oregon. An Englishman with a remote air, Alexander, I thought, was a bit overbearing, but deeply spiritual — a man who had come to God and made His message the priority of his life.

I learned from Alexander how to center, to meditate and understand that God is everywhere and that I am part of Everything.

For me that was a magnificent revelation and a reassurance that I was more than myself.

In the intervening years, I have dwelled on the lessons of love, life and light Alexander has taught and I have learned that I am more human than I thought and I overcame my apathy and arrived at a perspective of life, both before and after the flesh, that convinced me of a destination for my soul that may be beyond the stars and certainly beyond the horizons we plain people use as measures of our stature and vision.

Alexander gives us inspiration, truth about who we ultimately are and boldly challenges us to accept the idea of human divinity. It was my pleasure to help him bring his book to completion.

THORN BACON

Chapter One

Oneness

No man is an island unto himself
We are all a piece of the continent.

John Donne

It seems proper in this first chapter that I should introduce myself so that you can become acquainted with my personal history and how I came to answer for myself the question, Who am I? It is this singular question with which this book is absorbed. It is a question I hope to help you answer for yourself.

The urgency and depth of this question was expressed with remarkable insight several years ago by Ravi Ravindra who understood the deep frustration, the loneliness, the misery and the frightening isolation that we humans experience when we begin to ask of ourselves probing questions about our origin, our purpose on this planet and our future when we leave it.

Ravindra, a celebrated professor of Religion and Physics at Dalhousie University, Halifax, Nova Scotia, describes the human dilemma when he observes:

"What am I asking when I ask Who am I? What sort of answer would be acceptable? Do I want a chart of my genealogical and social relations? A list of my racial and biological characteristics? A catalogue of my psychological features — my likes and dislikes, desires and fears? These are all the things that shape my personality. But whose personality is it? Who wears this mask? In response to a little knock at the door of my consciousness, I ask Who is it? No naming — son of God, Self, Atman, 'Buddha' — is sufficient. What I seek is to see the face of the one who calls.

"Who Am I? does not ask for an enumeration of scientific facts: it expresses a certain restlessness, groping, and exploration. It is the beginning of a movement toward light, toward seeing things clearly, as a whole. It is the refusal to remain in the dark — fragmented and on the surface of myself. It is a state of searching for meaning, comprehensiveness and depth. It is the desire to wake up."

It is the desire to wake up which has prompted you, the reader, to purchase this book and seek personal answers which you hope it may contain. Answers which may illuminate your ignorance of who you are, why you are here and why you do what you do.

Deeply aware of this hunger for self recognition, Ravindra observes:

"All spiritual traditions thus diagnose the human condition: man is asleep and his life — ambitions, fears, activities — are governed by vast forces, outside of his will or control. He can, with instruction, grace, and effort, wake up, see his situation as it is, and begin to listen to his inner voice."

My message, then, expressed as *Inward Bound,* is a
wake-up call to self knowledge, and it was Ravindra, wise
about the groping for enlightenment, who wrote that:

"Self realization is the main theme of all the
Upanishads. (The *Upanishads* are part of the ancient Hindu
Vedic Scriptures.) 'He who knows that which is set in the
secret place of the heart, he here on earth, O beloved, casts
asunder the knot of ignorance.'"

This sage of the late twentieth century, who has spent
a lifetime penetrating the veil that shields the spirit, touches
the mystery of human nature when he writes about the
"hidden" in us:

"However, this hidden one is not easily assigned a
place. In a deep experience of listening or seeing, what is
outside us is also inside. We ourselves are as mysterious as
the kingdom and may hold the keys to it. If we can open the
doors of the interior castle, the king might come and sit on
the throne."

It is to this interior castle that I wish to lead readers. In
fact, it appears that the only way to God is self-knowing,
dying to outer self, and being born to a deeper inner self.
There are clearly differences in detail and emphasis, but
there is no other point on which there is a greater unanimity
of principle among the various masters of spiritual
becoming. Spiritual becoming is the path to the interior
castle which searchers of the self eventually find. It is
another name for the Divine consciousness, which one may
only recognize when he penetrates the nature of his own
soul.

Of course what Ravindra takes us to is the admission
that "within ourselves at the level of ordinary humanity,
where we usually are, there is confusion and chaos.... Only
deeper down, is there the possibility of increased under-

standing, integration and wholeness. Only in a state of collectedness, composure, openness, and alertness can we know anything objectively. In all other states our perceiving apparatus is out of tune and introduces its own noise arising out of internal or external distractions and affliction. Nothing that we decipher in these dispersed states is ultimately trustworthy."

Ravindra's wisdom brings us to the main purpose of *Inward Bound,* which, like other spiritual ideas, I formed to help men and women repair and prepare themselves — to guide them into a state of new spiritual vigilance, freed of subjective desires, expectations and fears. For as long "as we keep making our little noises," as Ravindra notes, we truly cannot hear. Only when quietened within, may we encounter what is real. And that is one of the chief objectives of *Inward Bound* — on the way to a purified, integrated state of being.

Finding one's way into a purified state of being does not happen overnight. But that should never be an excuse to put off the self-discovery that leads to being an expanded human — the condition of increased understanding, composure, and openness, described as Oneness.

My own road to self-discovery started when I was a child in England when my father lost his fortune during the collapse of the London Stock Market that heralded the Great Depression of 1929.

Little did I suspect in those days that many years later I would be described in the book *Spirit of Champions* as "the Englishman who became a U.S. citizen and later founded Mind Dynamics. This was the organization responsible for turning out the people who started such famous human potential programs as est, The Forum, LifeSpring, Lifestream, Context Training, PSI Seminars, Personal

Dynamics of Switzerland, Life Dynamics of Japan, Alpha training seminars in Australia and many others.

"It is safe to say that Alexander Everett, with his ideas, his personality, the depth of his vision, was the innovator around whom the entire human movement of mental imagery in the United states was staged. He was the center, the inspiration, the thinker who had come from the British Isles. There he was a successful teacher who established Pendragon, a preparatory school in Sussex, England, after which he founded and became headmaster of Shiplake College. But money and high position were not enough for Alexander; he was stirred by a desire to help people clarify themselves, find themselves, discover who they were and how they fit into the world — into the universe."

Though Mind Dynamics was a financial success — I taught people how to think right, feel right, and act right — it was not enough for me. There were too many people who came to my workshops who failed to learn; they resisted change, returning to ingrained patterns of negativity soon after the "workshop glow" had worn off.

There had to be a better way, I realized, and I found it in the spiritual state of human consciousness. This state, as I have described, represents the God essence within each individual. It is the universal power, God, within each of us, whatever we choose to call it. And that part is perfect.

Looking back on my own life long before Mind Dynamics, and before my father lost his money, I remember the good times we had. My mother, father, sister and I made up a happy family of four. My father had an above-average income, so we lived in style. My sister and I were educated at private schools and knew the life of privilege and comfort. As a result of a wound in trench warfare that took an eye from my father during World War I, he could not get a driver's license. Consequently, we went everywhere by train or taxi and I well remember we not only traveled First Class, but were considered socially prominent. The station master would see us off, complete with his black top hat, at such train terminals as London's Victoria Station.

Our summer holidays were spent in a rented house at the seaside in Sussex on the south coast of England. Most of the year we lived in hotel suites; life was grand and wonderful until that day in 1929, when I was eight years old.

Just prior to that awful day, we had been living in Littlehampton, a seaside resort on the south coast of England. We had rooms in what was called 51 South Terrace. It was a private hotel, I think, because each floor had different people living on it, and there was a dining room downstairs. During that time, because my father was still well-to-do, he played golf every day on a golf course situated across the River Arun. He took a ferry across the river with other golfers, stepping out on the far shore for his game. Often I rode the ferry over and back, and it was an intriguing experience for me to watch the ferryman ply his oars against a strong river current.

At that time I went to a kindergarten run by the Misses Beebe, two sisters who seemed very ancient to me, but I don't suppose they really were. I remember thinking of them as polite refugees from the previous, musty decades, whose style, elegance and demeanor suggested a genteel Victorian past whose dominant color surely must have been mauve. I was never a very good student. At school we had to sit around a table and read and write. I was always looking out of the window, so the sisters made me stand in a corner. I'll always remember I got into big trouble because I used to lick the wallpaper as I stood in the corner. I can't remember why I should do such a thing. Maybe the dried paste tasted good.

At any rate, in those days telegrams were delivered by youths who wore leather belts with a pouch attached around their waists. One such young man called on us and took a telegram from his pouch. And that's when my father read the terrible news. He was ruined, hammered on the London Stock Exchange, unable to meet his commitments.

I don't know whether it's true or not, but the shock was so great that my mother's hair went gray overnight. And, of course, we went from being very wealthy to having absolutely nothing, paupers in a day. Everything was taken from us, everything. My father managed to find a place for us to live, a little rent home, a semi-detached house at 15 St. Flora's Road, Littlehampton.

There are two outstanding memories I have of those moneyless times. One is that we had an apple tree down in the garden. Beautiful red apples hung from the branches. My bedroom overlooked the apple tree, so one day I said to my father, "Let's pick the apples today."

"No, we'll wait one more day," he said. "They'll be ripe and perfect then."

I was eager to bite into a ripe pippen, so I was up early the next morning, hungry, my imagination painting the crisp sound of my crunching into a perfect apple. But when I looked out of the window, I stared at a bare tree. All the apples had been stolen during the night. I rushed downstairs and said to my mother grievously, "You know, someone has stolen all our apples in the night. Every one is gone."

She made a statement I've never forgotten: "Whoever took the apples, their need must be greater than ours."

I remember thinking, "Wow, what a charitable thing to say." That impressed me very much as a child.

The other thing I remember was that from our meager money my mother had saved a little for Christmas. She went shopping with her precious five-pound note and lost her purse at Woolworth's.

She came home and told my father that she'd lost the five pounds and our Christmas was ruined, just like that. I remember the silence. In the shared gloom, my sister and I, and my mother and father sat down for tea and bread and scrape (a paste made of lard that you scrape on the bread). We sat in absolute silence, very upset, shocked at our outrageous bad fortune.

There was a knock on the door, and when my father opened it there was an old man standing in the doorway. He had found my mother's purse at Woolworth's. Her name and address were in it and he had brought it back. We gave him a ten-shilling note, the equivalent of ten percent of the five pounds. Of course, our whole attitude changed when we realized we could have a Christmas after all.

Many things became very obvious to me at that time of my life. We had nothing, but we were much closer together than ever before. We had bicycles, we certainly didn't have a car, and we used to go to the beach and picnicking in the country. We picked daffodils and bluebells in the woods in the spring. It was a very together time in my life, because we were so poor. But some sacrifices were beyond the charity of a nine-year-old: I refused to wear my mother's shoes when mine wore out. When my shoes finally gave up the ghost, I told my mother I couldn't go to school. "My shoes are falling apart."

"You can wear my flat heeled shoes," she urged.

I said no. I wasn't going to wear a woman's shoes to school. We had a terrific argument but I stayed away from school — I refused to go.

It wasn't long after that my mother's parents asked us to move in with them at Harpenden. This was in 1934. They had a big home, which was built in 1932. My grandparents were quite pious and reserved Sunday for worship at church and at home. So devout were they that they closed the heavy drapes over the windows in their house to preserve the seclusion and privacy of the holy day. My grandfather died the same year. My father was able to support us from a job he got in the business my grandfather had started. The company was named Douglas Stratford and Co., an auctioneer and estate agent business.

Thanks to my grandmother things improved for us at Harpenden. She paid for me to go to boarding school, and I was shipped back to Littlehampton because the man who ran the school there was a friend of my father's. The school was called Dorset House, and I attended for two years, until I was thirteen. This school still exists to this day near by at the manor in Bury, Sussex.

It was at Littlehampton that I had my vision. It was, I think, as I reflected on it later, an inspiration that deeply affected my life and set a course for me I didn't fully appreciate at the time.

My vision happened at our parish church, the Church of England, where we went for matins at eleven o'clock every Sunday morning. One Sunday, a bishop from Africa, a black man, gave the sermon. He was very tall, six feet, six inches, with a big crook in his hand and lofty miter on his head, very impressive to a child. He stood up in the pulpit, gave a sermon, and I never took my eyes off him — I was so amazed. After he finished his sermon, he went up to the altar to bless the collection money, and at that time when he held up his hands facing the altar with his back to us, I had a strong vision of myself as a minister, a teacher and a spiritual leader. I saw myself like the bishop who stood at the altar. This image came very clear to my mind, and it surprised me. I was only about twelve.

My vision prompted me to go to a shop that sold religious things, where I bought two miniature brass candlesticks, three inches tall. I bought birthday cake candles, and I had a little statue of Jesus.

On the mantlepiece above the fireplace in my bedroom, I placed the statue of Jesus, the candles and a cross, too. When my parents discovered my altar and the religious objects, they looked surprised, they couldn't understand my sudden devoutness. At the time I installed my altar, my mother was subscribing to an American magazine called *Daily Word.* Apparently, she was one of the first subscribers in England. It was published by the Unity School of Christianity. It had a very drab, brown cover; not a very exciting magazine, but she read it every day.

I imagine I must have read it, for I asked if there was a magazine for children. Soon, I received a magazine called *Weekly Unity.* It had a five-cent stamp on it from America. I was very excited about it. I remember reading *Unity,* which seemed to bolster my vision, and it wasn't long after that I quit eating meat. My reading room at boarding school was in the basement with the coke fueled boiler, where my concentration and privacy would be undisturbed by school chums. My parents were not happy about my decision to refrain from meat, but I did it anyhow. I just told them that I was at the age when I could make decisions. So, at Littlehampton, I had the vision, built the altar, and I started subscribing to *Unity* magazine. And that's why, when eventually I came to America, I sought out Unity. It was a natural step leading from my powerful vision.

I've been asked about the precocious age at which I saw my vision. And, of course, parents are bewildered by strange behavior from their children. Mine were no different. They didn't understand, but I remember thinking that my vision was not unusual. Children take such happenings as a matter of course. Their innocence and receptivity to secret voices and invisible images is still intact. They do not have the fear of the unexplained that adults do, nor their superstitions.

It is true that, at the time, I was certain I was going to be a minister. Later, when I got older and read the 39 articles of the Church of England, I could not accept the beliefs they embraced.

I moved from childhood into my teens, a secret rebel who had become deeply moved by the cherished image of my early vision. I matured with my vision and perhaps because of it avoided many of the intellectual distortions of the teen-age years. It is surprising how early I rejected the sterile and guarded forms of private and public education as restrictive, pompous and unimaginative. By the time I was 16, I was in full revolt, demanding freedom from class-rooms.

At Harpenden, where the family lived thanks to the generosity of my grandmother, there was a happening I'll always remember with fond nostalgia. We still had lamplighters in those days. A man mounted on a bicycle came every night and stopped in front of our house as part of his route. Like a dutiful sentry, I used to watch out for him with my face pressed against the window pane. He had a long stick attached to which was a chain that he pulled to make the street light go on — it was gas, I suppose. I thought how charming and dependable that mysterious, endearing man was, and yet I knew — I don't know how — that he would disappear. The world was changing. It wasn't long after my vigils for the lamplighter that a popular song came over the radio. It was called "The Old Lamplighter," and I thought it was written about the colorful figure who came to light up our neighborhood.

Teaching changed my earlier dream of becoming a minister when I left school at 16. I was very upset about school and, because I disliked it so much, I said to myself that one day I'd have my own school and I'd run it differently. Well, at this time, there was a little prep school for young boys aged six to thirteen. It was called Moreton End, not far away from where we lived. They used to play soccer on a field close by and I watched them practice sometimes.

One day the man coaching the team commented that I came often to watch. I affirmed his observation, and I said I liked soccer a lot. He asked if I'd like to help him, and I said, "Sure."

"Can you be here tomorrow?" he asked. "Can you run the program? I have to go somewhere."

Well, I did run the game. I was 16 and I could do anything. I was successful. And then one day the headmaster's wife came to see me. She asked if I would like to help at the school on a permanent basis.

That was the beginning. Then Mr. O'Hara, the headmaster, died suddenly of cancer, and the school was shorthanded. I was asked to take over the coaching. I was only 17 and I got my first experience of teaching school. Then, of course, the war came and that put an end to that. But I was well on my way to becoming a teacher. I knew that was what I wanted to do.

I remember another time, a Sunday afternoon, we were in the garden at home. Neville Chamberlain, our Prime Minister, announced on the radio that England was at war with Germany. The date was September 3, 1939. I'll always remember the solemnity in his voice as we sat out in the garden. I think it was about three o'clock in the afternoon. We had tea, and my father made no comment, because, you see, he'd fought in the First World War, and was upset that this should happen again so soon. I have to admit I was more interested in spiritual matters than the war, for I had met a man, John Moreton, who was to become a big influence in my life.

I can't remember exactly how I met Moreton, but it must have been in his bookshop. I had developed an interest in metaphysical books, and it drew me to Moreton's bookshop on Great Russell Street right next to the British Museum in London. Moreton, a man in his sixties was the proprietor of the shop. The walls of the store were decorated with some very unusual paintings all done in colors of the rainbow. Very beautiful — sunsets, ocean scenes and abstracts — very beautiful to me.

Moreton must have seen how eager I was to learn, and we became friends. He'd recommend books for me to read, one of which, published in 1924, I still have. Its pages have yellowed now. The name of the book is *The Simple Way of Lao Tse,* which is a translation of the Tao Teh Ching. It is the story of the yin and yang, the circle and the balance of the two. Though the subject, on the surface, was removed from any consideration of the opposite sex, which was then the object of my growing interest, I did discover that life was a matter of balance — you couldn't be one without the other.

While my primary interest in the opposite sex was intellectual, I am sure it was hormonal as well. In my readings about the relationship between male and female, I found out that the male was the outgoing activity and the female was the incoming, intuitive part. The more I read and the more I looked at my own life, the more I realized that I needed to bring a romantic balance into it.

I wasn't very interested in marrying at that time, but I remember I met a girl, who lived next door, actually. I had dreamed of one day marrying her, but I was still young. I became upset when she met someone at the beginning of the war, a young fellow in the military, an officer. He was gallant in his uniform and she decided to marry him. Because we were neighbors, I was invited to the wedding. She was a very young girl, in her teens when she got married, about the same age as I. Peter, her husband-to-be, was somewhat older than she. She asked me to be the best man.

"Pamela Ann," I said, "It's not for you to choose. It's Peter's decision."

"Well, then you can be an usher."

Her husband, Peter Carter-Ruck, later turned out to be a very brilliant lawyer. After the war, we got to be good friends, and I visited him in London. He developed fame as a libel lawyer, and became very wealthy. He's always been a steadfast friend of mine. Peter assisted me greatly in the founding of Shiplake College. Without him I doubt if the college would have been formed.

I came to understand a lot about balance later, but very little then. As an adolescent at 17, though precocious perhaps about my grasp of spirituality, I did some strange things. I wore clothes that were a bit different, like kids nowadays. I remember I had an overcoat. It was huge, it went almost down to my ankles. And I loved it. My parents looked at me as if I were from another planet. It was that period of youth when I wanted to create my own identity.

Those of us who understand early in their years, as I did, the absolute necessity to grope and find their purpose in life have launched themselves on a journey that will take them ever deeper inward bound. And, of course, with the foregoing observations I have recorded here, it is that journey that I ask you to to take with me, step by step, into your future.

You will remember that I introduced you to Ravi Ravindra at the beginning of this chapter. I think it is fitting that I call on him for concluding words about the journey into Self:

"When we thus know ourselves, we no longer know *this* self or *that* self; we know the Self, unrestricted by any particularity. This knowledge is possible only when one's my-ness, one's ego is transcended. Strictly speaking, therefore, there is no one who is anyone who knows the Self; the Self knows itself. This is what Plotinus calls 'a flight of the Alone to the Alone.' 'Not I, the I that I am, know these things,' says Jacob Boehme, 'but God knows them in me.' It is this self into which we who labor and are heavy laden must go to find rest. If, abandoning all else, in this alone we take refuge, we shall be released from evil."

"We only know ourselves when one's my-ness, one's ego is transcended...." these words composed by Ravindra, and paraphrased by other philosophers and spiritual leaders, lead us to the concept of oneness — that state of living I described earlier: oneness — which reflects increased understanding, integration and wholeness.

I believe the person who comprehends oneness is like the listener who hears the quiet, steady voice within himself say, "To live, work and suffer on this shore in faithfulness to the whispers from the other shore is spiritual life."

Oneness is the power with which each of us is born, and which we strive to recognize as we seek to define our humanity and our eternity. And yet the signs of oneness are all about us. Reflecting back on my own childhood, I see in retrospect the oneness of my family.

The symbol for oneness is a circle, which has no beginning or end. Three dimensionally, a circle becomes a sphere. The earth that we live on is a sphere, which means we all need to live in a state of oneness.

As you mature you may reach that stage in life where you will wish to create your own family. You meet a person with whom you want to form a partnership for life. You decide to get married. Now there is a very important part of the wedding ceremony, called the exchange of rings. The ring is shaped in the form of a circle and represents oneness. When the two exchange rings, the two become one.

For the rest of your lives the rings on your fingers will remind you that the two of you are forever one. I often wonder how it is, that once the ring ceremony has been completed, and the marriage vows made that two people could ever seek a separation or a divorce.

The answer seems to be that they never truly accepted and recognized the bond of oneness between the two of them. If they had connected in the first place at a deeper spiritual level, the bond of oneness would remain forever. In a true marriage, a third energy comes into being that unites the couple together for eternity. Strong words, you may say. However, the truth is that when two come together at the inner spiritual level, nothing will separate them.The deeper the connection, the more lasting the relationship. Real relationships are based on the power of oneness — which only occurs at the spiritual level — and once that oneness has been forged, the ring on the finger no longer remains just a symbol. It becomes the unifying force that holds the two together for the rest of their lives. It was a great philosopher who wrote, "When the one man loves the one woman and the one woman loves the one man, the very angels leave heaven and come and sit in that house and sing for joy."

It is interesting to note that the origin of the ring ceremony we use in the wedding ceremony dates back many years to the early church and is still used in certain religious orders. For example, when a nun takes her vows, a ceremony is performed in which the ring is used to illustrate the nun's vows of oneness with God.

The power of oneness within the family is not a difficult concept to accept, but how about expanding this idea to the realm of the business world? How do you bring oneness into the marketplace? At first, this idea seems unlikely, since we have been brought up to think of business as being based on competition, which does not show much oneness toward the competition. But realize it or not, the ways of the world are changing. If you want to be successful you must substitute the word cooperation for competition and practice the art and power of oneness.

When I was younger and a school teacher, I founded and became the first headmaster of Shiplake College in England. In the early sixties, I came to the United States and helped to start another private school in Fort Worth, Texas. Then, for a couple of years, before I started to teach adults, I went into the restaurant business in Fort Worth. I noticed that on the street where I had my restaurant there were other types of food outlets selling hamburgers, Mexican food, pizza, fish and chips, steak and potatoes, and Italian food, just to name a few.

I visited all these different eating establishments and suggested that together we place a full-page advertisement in the *Fort Worth Star Telegram* describing our different styles of eating houses all on the same street. Instead of being "Automobile Row" this would be "Restaurant Row."

I met with much resistance, but eventually the plan was accepted and the bringing together of all the different types of restaurants was achieved. Each and every one of us benefited from this example of the power of oneness and increased our profits by leaps and bounds.

To expand on this concept, you will now find that many new shopping malls have food courts. In Eugene, Oregon, near where I live, the Valley River Center recently built a food court that displays every conceivable type of fast food outlet, all working together as one cohesive unit, even sharing the same tables and chairs for their customers. If you want to succeed, you should use your power of oneness. In fact, the very concept of a shopping mall is based on oneness. Each shop provides its own service and products in the one place where everybody comes to shop.

Your power of oneness can be portrayed as the win–win concept, which replaces the old idea of win–lose. In the past, a salesman made as much profit as possible at the expense of the buyer, who too often became a loser. Now with the win–win idea in action, both the buyer and the seller win. In making a deal you make sure that the two of you make a fair profit, thus both parties involved in the transaction are winners.

This works for me in my own life. I lecture and teach seminars all over the world, some years in as many as eight different countries. My sponsors add up the gross receipts and divide the proceeds by two, so that the sponsor and I each receive the same amount of money. Then each of us pays his own expenses.

Finally, your power of oneness can be shared with people you meet on the street and rub shoulders with in the course of daily living. From now on instead of seeing yourself as separate from others, realize you are one with all people, whoever they may be, or wherever you meet them. The truth is, we are all one. There is a simple rule you can adopt on a daily basis. Start to work with the "Golden Rule." In other words, do unto others as you would have them do unto you. This means doing simple things like opening a door for someone else, help carry parcels to a person's car, say a kind word, smile and be polite. Watch your driving habits by not cutting in front of another car.

If this all sounds very easy, yes it is. You will be amazed how your day goes better if you practice such simple, courteous behavior when you come in contact with other people. Now you must remember, you do this with everybody, both young and old, male and female, rich and poor, whatever background or culture a person comes from.

Now, it is timely for me to relate the concept of oneness to the Perennial Philosophy. Incidentally, a book with this title was written by an Englishman, Aldous Huxley, some fifty years ago.

Study of the world's religions reveals that there are certain underlying truths that are a part of every religious philosophy. The religions may appear to be different because they come from varied cultures, use unfamiliar names and have symbols of oneness to which we are not accustomed, but the essence of the teachings is identical. Nearly everything that Jesus said in the New Testament can be found in the Tao Teh Ching from China and the Bhagavad Gita from India. Jesus really said nothing new, but just in a way that was appropriate for his day and age.

So there's this perennial knowledge that every so many hundreds of years is revived by some teacher, religion or philosophy.

And do you know what? I have nothing new to tell you because it has all been told before. What I *can* do is to present it in a way you can understand better.

What is the meaning of "Perennial Philosophy?" Usually, we associate the word "perennial" with plants. For example, if we plant a seed that is an annual, it grows out of the ground, it flowers, and it dies all within a year. If we plant a biennial, it does not grow very much the first year. The second year it is really beautiful, and the third year it is no more. If we plant a perennial, it grows bigger and bigger each year, and never really dies, provided we divide the plant and give it room to grow.

The word "philosophy" comes from the Greek: *philos* means mental love, and *sophia,* wisdom. *Philosophy* literally means the love of wisdom. Put together, this is what "Perennial Philosophy" is all about. It is a knowledge that has always been and always will be.

First of all, the basic truth of this teaching is that there is a universal power. This power has a number of names: God, Yahweh, Brahman,Tao, Allah, or Almighty, but these are just labels for the power. God can be identified as a "person" or a principle, but the higher teachings look upon God as a principle that permeates all life. Secondly, the major religions also teach that man has a dual nature. He has the higher self and the lower self. Though the religions may give them different names, they are very clear about this duality.

Thirdly, religions state that it is only through the higher self that we can make the connection with God.

The fourth, and most powerful teaching of all: the purpose of life is to make this connection and to let the higher, eternal self become one with the God-self. To help us in this process, God incarnates as a man, comes into this realm and re-ignites this Perennial Philosophy when humanity falls to a lower state of consciousness. It is not that we are not all children of God, but we need help at times through great teachers and avatars. An avatar knows who he is at birth, and knows the teaching he has come to bring.

Jesus was an avatar: he was a great teacher. At twelve years of age, he went to the temple and amazed the priests, and at that time he knew who he was. Sai Baba is the one man on the planet today that we know to be an avatar. He also knew his calling at twelve years of age when he told his family, "I am Sai Baba," and started performing miracles. By the time he was a teenager, he had formed a group of followers. From the insights of avatars, religions and teachings now are created by the followers to carry on the work, and, to repeat, *the basic teachings, which are the same.*

For example, go back to the earliest known religion, Hinduism. Krishna was one of its early teachers, and he lived around 1200 BC. He made this statement: the Atman (the individual soul) and the Brahman (the creator) are one. In other words, you need to become conscious that your higher self (your atman) is truly one with the God-self (Brahman).

Six hundred years after Krishna, in 600 BC, there were several avatars on earth at the same time: Buddha, Confucius, Lao Tse, and others. Buddha is probably the best known, so we will look at the focus of his teachings as representative of the group. Buddha said, "If you look within, you will see thou art the Buddha." Then Jesus, another 600 years later in AD 30, said, "The kingdom of heaven is within." And 600 years after Jesus, in AD 600, Muhammad said, "When you know yourself, you know the

Lord," which he called Allah. This Atman, this Buddha, this Heaven, this Self, this whatever-you-want-to-call-it, is within you. This, your higher self, needs to be realized and to be one with God.

One of my main principles of teaching is that what I am teaching has been known for eons. I'm only reviving it. I love living now because I can teach once more these great perennial truths that have always existed and will continue to exist.

There is another doctrine that is part of this Perennial Philosophy. Once humanity was in a higher state of consciousness, and we are now returning to that state. We are not evolving to be greater beings. We are *revolving,* returning, being born again to that which we once were. We are coming again to oneness. This is a period of renaissance. The stories and myths of each religion indicate this very truth.

Consider the Christian teaching of the prodigal son. The story goes that a young man asks his father for his inheritance so that he can use it while he is still young. (An interesting point is that the father does not question the son, but gives the money to him.) The son goes off and has fun doing whatever they did in those days to squander a fortune. The son becomes penniless. He ends up getting a job feeding pigs.

It suddenly occurs to him that his father's servants are better off than he is. He decides to go home and to ask for forgiveness. He starts on the journey, and halfway there his father meets him and welcomes him with gifts: a ring to put on his finger, a cloak to place around his shoulders, and shoes for his feet. These gifts symbolize returning to the knowledge of who he once was. The ring, the circle of oneness, symbolizes returning to oneness. His cloak is the robe of knowledge, rather like the gown students wear at graduation, and the shoes symbolize understanding. The shoes clothe the feet on which we stand, thus representing our foundation of understanding.

The question arises: When did we have this consciousness and how did we lose it? Again, there is a mythological story in every religion that tells of this event. The story of the flood involves a catastrophe where almost everyone dies except for a remnant of survivors. The catastrophe happened when man misused this inner power. It seems that humanity became so powerful when it awoke to this God-power that it misused it. "Power corrupts, and total power corrupts totally." Thus we have the story of the fall of Atlantis as well as the story of the flood. These stories indicate that man misused his God-powers, lost them, and had to start all over again.

And ever since the fall, we have been recovering the awareness of who we are; we have been separated from the knowledge of this incredible power. We are now recovering this knowledge. Individually, people are waking up.

Every one of you to some degree, is a prodigal child. You've all misused your powers and are now waking up and saying, "I want to go home." Why do you think you are reading this book? Because you are on your way home to the realization of who you really are, to an understanding of the concept of oneness. And maybe I have something to help you to go home ... to help you to go back and to live in that higher state of oneness and togetherness.

You have a gift and a power within you, that when you wake up to it and let the Atman become one with the Brahman, or you enter the Kingdom of Heaven, or you realize you are the Buddha, when you understand all of that, you can stand up and be counted, and make a difference in the world.

And that's what I'm here to do. That's my mission. That's the "Perennial Philosophy." You are an integral, inseparable part of it.

To sum up the concept of oneness, once you begin to practice it from your heart you will go:

From controlling others	~	to loving others.
From exploiting others	~	to serving others.
From competition	~	to cooperation.
From win–lose	~	to win–win.
From acquiring	~	to giving.
From owning	~	to sharing.
From personal self	~	to universal Self.
From separation	~	to oneness.

Chapter Two

Duality and Balance

Yang is the power to give
Yin is the power to receive.

Lao Tse

The symbol of yang and yin represents the interaction between the male outgoing love and the female incoming intuition. You will see how yin and yang are exemplified in the following story.

In the early 1960s I flew to Inverness in the north of Scotland to visit with Peter Caddy and his wife Eileen. Caddy, an ex-RAF squadron leader turned hotelkeeper, and his intuitive wife, had settled on hostile, barren land barely three miles from the battlements of Duncan's Castle at Forres. Just their scrap of land was south of the heath where it was prophesied by the three witches in Shakespeare's Macbeth that he would be thane of Glamis and Cawdor.

In this raw, windblown and romantic setting a
modern miracle was performed at Findhorn, an unsightly,
overcrowded encampment of mobile homes, and an
unlikely place for Caddy who once walked two thousand
miles through the Himalayas, crossing Kashmir deep into
Tibet. His physical appearance was more that of a gentle-
manly country squire, than a hard-handed, round-shoul-
dered farmer stooped from years of labor in the soil. Ten
years after my visit, Peter Tomkins and Christopher Bird
in their book *The Secret Life of Plants,* described the
wonderful gardening experiment performed by Caddy and
his wife Eileen, along with a friend, Dorothy Maclean
from Canada.

"For some time," the authors explain, "the Caddys had
been intent upon radically changing their lives by turning
away from mundane occupations and materialist pursuits in
order to enter upon what Caddy calls a long period of
training and preparation. During this period they planned to
surrender everything, including all personal volition, to a
being they term 'Unlimited Power and Love,' whose will is
manifest to them through the guidance of a deceased
Rosicrucian master whom they recognized in the flesh as
Dr. G. A. Sullivan, and in the spirit as Aureolus, or St.
Germain, or the Master of the Seventh Ray.

"To be fair, the place in which the Caddys least
expected to settle was … known as Findhorn Caravan Park.
For years they had hurried past it on their way to and from
Forres. Now some mysterious force was overriding their
aversion. Following what appeared to be crystal guidance,
they wheeled an old caravan onto the site of their new home
— less than half an acre in a hollow not far from the main
cluster of trailers, a patch of land composed mainly of sand
and gravel, constantly swept by gale-force winds, protected

only partially by tufts of broom and quitch grass which kept
the sand from blowing away, and shaded by a belt of spiny
fir trees."

I learned from Caddy the heroic effort they expended
in their adventure on the wind-swept land, but as Tompkins
and Bird write, "Following the concept of the monks who
used to build their monasteries by hand, putting love and
light into the fabric of the building with every stone they
laid, the Caddys cleaned their rickety trailer from top to
bottom and polished all the furniture, pouring in vibrations
of love to cancel out the negative vibrations they considered
to be inevitable in structures built by people interested only
in money. Cleansing and hand painting the caravan was a
first step toward the creation of their own center of light."

It was to Eileen, with her practice of going within, that
Peter Caddy looked to for guidance, for she was a remarkable woman, a sensitive, who rose regularly from her bed at
midnight and meditated for several hours. Wrapping herself
in a thick overcoat to protect her against the sharp, invasive
cold of Scottish nights, she secluded herself in the trailer
park's freezing toilet. It was the only place in the camp
where Eileen could find absolute tranquility. There, she
opened her mind and spirit to communications from Devas
or angelic creatures who controlled the spirits that managed
the world of nature.

Revealed to Eileen in a very clear vision were seven
cedarwood bungalows placed together in a cluster. They
surrounded a magnificent garden, trim, neat and blooming
with vegetables and flowers. Eileen was unconcerned about
how her vision was to materialize on a hard plot of ground
on which nothing grew but tough, pointed grass. To make
matters worse, the soil was composed of fine, dusty sand
and gravel which was almost impervious to water.

Eileen explained to Peter that she had been instructed that each time he put a spade into the ground, he must put in with it his own loving vibrations, his good intentions. The right vibrations, Eileen said, would attract, like a magnet, other good vibrations.

On the strength of Eileen's direction, Peter Caddy prepared the stubborn soil for seeding, despite the fact that according to the local agricultural experts and textbooks on gardening, nothing could be grown in the Findhorn soil with the possible exception of a few scraggly radishes and lettuces — hardly the kind of robust fuel for the body the laboring couple required.

Within two months of the time Peter Caddy planted the garden, the results, according to authors Tompkins and Bird "… were stunning to the neighbors, who, not knowing of the spirit in which the Caddys were going about their gardening, could not understand what was happening, especially when the Caddys' cabbages and Brussels sprouts were the only ones in the area to survive a plague of cabbage-root grubs, which eat away at the roots of the plants, and their harvest of black currants grew healthily by the bushel, whereas the crop largely failed in the rest of the county.

"Findhorn lunches began to consist of salads with over twenty ingredients; surplus quantities of lettuce, radishes, spinach, and parsley were disposed of round the county, which was suffering a shortage. Their evening meals included two or three vegetables from the garden, grown without fertilizer or insecticides, freshly picked and freshly cooked. Stews from garden vegetables consisted of onions, leeks, garlic, carrots, parsnips, rutabagas, turnips, artichokes, kohlrabi, celery, squash, potatoes, flavored with all kinds of herbs."

By the time midsummer rolled around the novice gardeners were ready to preserve large quantities of blackberries, raspberries and strawberries. Altogether they put up more than 100 pounds of jam. When Peter Caddy turned to estimating the number of red cabbages the small group would require for the following winter season, he figured that with an average weight of three or four pounds they would need no more than eight heads.

To the Findhorners' amazement, as authors Tompkins and Bird report:

"... when the cabbages matured one of them weighed thirty-eight pounds and another forty-two. A sprouting broccoli, mistakenly planted as a cauliflower, grew to such enormous proportions that it provided vegetables for weeks; when eventually pulled out of the ground it was nearly too heavy to be lifted."

To what arcane power could the growth of such gigantic plants be credited? When Peter Caddy finally released the secret of the Findhorn gardeners he said Eileen and Dorothy Maclean had made direct contact with angelic creatures, the ones who control the nature spirits who are described by clairvoyants to be at work everywhere nurturing plant life.

From Dorothy Maclean came the exciting disclosure that she had received messages directly from plant world spirits giving specific instructions on how the gardeners would plant and care for the seeds, growing vegetables and flowers.

Suddenly, Findhorn, the windblown garden of magnificence in a remote, cold corner of northern Scotland, became famous overnight. What had begun as a small garden to nourish a few sensitive people, "... appeared to be turning into a true center of light for the Aquarian Age...."

Tompkins and Bird furnish the final comment on Findhorn:

"Parting the veil into other worlds and other vibrations beyond the limits of the electromagnetic spectrum may well go a long way to explain the mysteries which are incomprehensible to physicists who limit their looking to what they can see with their physical eyes and their instruments. In the more ethereal world of the clairvoyant, who claims to have mastered the art of etheric and astral vision, a whole new series of vistas opens up around plants and their relation to man, to the earth, and to the cosmos. The growth of seed and plants, as Paracelsus intimated, may indeed be affected very strongly by the position of the moon, the positions of the planets, their relation to the sun and to the other stars of the firmament."

To this I add the comment of Dr. Aubrey Westlake, the author of *Pattern of Health,* who describes our imprisoned state:

"We are locked in a valley of materialistic concepts, refusing to believe there is anything other than the physical–material world of our five senses. For we, like the inhabitants of the country of the blind, reject those who claim to have 'seen' with their spiritual vision the greater supersensible world in which we are immersed, dismissing such claims as 'idle fancies' and advancing far 'saner' scientific explanations."

Now that you've met the remarkable Caddys you can better understand the concept of balance, one of the major subjects of this chapter. Peter Caddy clearly demonstrated his understanding of the intuitive nature of his wife. It was she, who sat quietly and focused inwardly, who was the message receiver from the Devic world of nature spirits.

To her, and Dorothy Maclean, they gave instructions for the cultivation and care of the garden at Findhorn. And it was the two women who passed what they learned to Peter

Caddy who acted physically to make Findhorn a grand experiment, to create a vegetable, fruit and flower kingdom, in love, acknowledgement of God, and simple compliance to the duality represented by male and female in partnership. The intuitive woman together with the active physical man created a marvelous balance, which is the rule of life.

By living in balance not only can you avoid unpleasant distortions in your life, but you can open yourself to opportunities that will improve your joy and understanding of life.

Living in balance is incredibly important. It embraces how you deal with money, food, exercise — how you deal with life. The best way to explain what I mean is to tell you what I do myself. That does not mean that you should do exactly what I do. Nevertheless, you need to look at balance as I will discuss it. Understand the point I am making, and work to establish your own balance in your own way, if you want to have a longer-lasting, happier life.

Much of what I have learned has been through experimentation. For instance, when I was young I thought the big issue was to have money. I followed that direction, and I made a considerable amount of money. I founded two successful private boys' schools in England. I owned a forty-room home, and a car that goes with that style of living. But my life was very much out of balance. It did not work; it did not give me what I thought it would.

Because I was still fairly young, aged forty to be exact, I decided perhaps the opposite direction would be better. I made my school into a charitable trust and gave the property to the nation. I came to America with a few dollars in my pocket and went to work for Unity School of Christianity. I had no possessions at all — not even a car. In my mind, I was doing without to become more spiritual.

But I found that being poor did not work, either. So I eventually received the message that there is a balance that allows a person to have a car, clothes and a home, but without being greedy and trying to make millions of dollars.

That experience taught me that living in balance is of the utmost importance. To this day, I follow the middle path. I do not seek a fortune nor wish to be poor. I live in the country, and, since there is only one of me, I built my own one-room house. I own a car and live comfortably. My aim is to live in a simple manner so that others can simply live.

Now, let's examine another area of life, diet. When I was twelve years old, I had a terrific impulse that I should not eat meat. I did not understand why at the time, but I knew that this was what I should do. Everybody thought I was a little crazy, but I stuck to my convictions.

As I grew older, I centered myself and went within to find the things that work for me. At first I thought the same things should be right for everybody, but I have learned that each person has his own rhythm that he must find. For example, one of the things that my body does not tolerate is excessive sweetness in foods. I remember when I went to boarding school as a child they served brown bread with honey as a special treat on Thursday afternoon. Edith was the matron (I can see her now!), and she used to put dollops of honey on large slices of brown bread. I would say, "I don't want it!" And she would say, "You have to eat it. It's good for you!" And I would say, "I'll get sick if I do." I found I couldn't swallow sweet food. And to this day I still do not eat honey, but most people do with no ill effects.

Through the years, I have found that simplicity is the best way for me. I learned from Harvey and Marilyn Diamond's book, *Fit for Life,* to have fruit juice in the morning, and for lunch I make what I call a smoothie: I blend an apple, banana and grape juice. Then at dinner, lots of salad in the summer and a plate piled high with steamed vegetables in the winter. This is what works for me.

I have learned from other people's examples, too. I read John Robbin's book, *Diet for a New America,* and as a result have given up animal fat altogether. I was already a vegetarian, so I was halfway there. But I liked grated hard cheese or cottage cheese on my vegetables. When I became serious about not eating animal fat, I discovered a wonderful margarine made out of soybeans. I put this on my vegetables instead of cheese, and it has a great flavor. I toss everything into the pot — potatoes, carrots, broccoli (you name it!) and steam them, and then put the soy margarine on top and it is delicious.

I am gradually working out what is right for me. But I would never want to impose that on other people. People want to know what I do, and I tell them, but you need to find what works best for you.

Another area that is important is exercise. Again, when I was young, I got hooked on having a strong, healthy body, and I exercised and did all the things necessary to do so. And then, when I was older, I went in the opposite direction and quit exercising, and that did not work either. Instinctively, I realized that somewhere along the line I had to have a balance regarding exercise as well.

I started reading books on aerobics, in particular *Fit or Fat* by Covert Bailey, and decided that jogging was the way to go. After all, I live near Eugene, Oregon, and that is the jogging capital of America! So I went out and bought a pair of jogging shoes — New Balance, right! — and started jogging on a daily basis. But there were times when the weather was bad, and the road conditions were sometimes dangerous with the logging trucks sweeping by, so I thought, "Maybe there's another way." Ask and you receive.

I had always resisted anything to do with machines. It did not make sense to me to ride a bicycle fixed to the floor, to do all that work and go nowhere, but I started experimenting anyway. A stationary bicycle did not work, and neither did a cross-country skiing machine. Then I was in the exercise room at Rosario Resort on Orcas Island at Love, Light and Life one day. A young student of mine, Eric — no more that sixteen — showed me a rowing machine, an ergometer that really appealed to me. So I bought one the next year and exercise with it for thirty minutes every day. It is great!

But I travel a great deal, and it occurred to me that I cannot take my rowing machine with me when I travel. So now I have been reading about the advantages of skipping rope. I have bought myself a skipping rope because I can take that with me and can skip rope anywhere I go in the world.

I hope you see the pattern here. You have to experiment to find the right balance for yourself! Something might not work, but one thing leads to another, and, when you center and go within, you will be led to what is right for you.

There is another major part of living in balance that I have left until last. I think it is the most important of all.

I teach that your work is, or should be, your pleasure. I enjoy teaching. But when I travel long distances to other countries, stay in hotels, teach and meet with people, it uses up a lot of energy. So what do I do to balance my life? I love nature and animals, so I bought twenty-five acres in the country and raise deer and donkeys, dogs and cats, and swans and ducks. I call my place "Animal Paradise." I have

found that this works incredibly well for me. I do both of
the things I love seven days a week. I live half of my life on
the road teaching people, and the other half at home with
nature and animals. This creates balance for me. Every one
of you — I do not care who you are or what you do — needs
to find a balance in your life. It might be a hobby, like
gardening or carpentry, but something you enjoy doing to
balance with your daily work.

I never teach anything unless I have done it myself. I
teach you how to center because I do it myself. I teach you
how to become a vegetarian because I am one. We learn
from each other — by our examples, not by what we say. To
make a difference in the world, you need to be an example.
You teach your children, you teach your friends, your
neighbors, by how you live. They do not remember what
you say, but rather who and how you are. Lead by example
— that is the best way to teach living in balance.

So, there you have it ... the tools you need to become
all that you can be to fulfill your birthright. Only you can
act upon them.

How long will it take? Exactly as long as you think it
will! If you start the process by centering every day, it will
happen sooner than you think. You'll learn about centering
in Chapter Ten of this book. But all the wisdom of the
universe will come to naught if it is not acted on.

The idea of balance extends far beyond man and
woman, you and me. The concept is at the heart of the
alignment of the world with universal energy. In the next
few pages we are going to look at the evidence of realign-
ment in our world and how it is producing a change in
energy on our planet.

The earth moves in three distinct cycles at the same
time. First, it revolves on its axis every twenty-four hours,

creating night and day. The sun is the earth's energy source, so we need to get up when it rises, be active while it is shining and go to sleep when it is dark. "Early to bed and early to rise makes a man healthy, wealthy and wise," is an axiom of correct living. The worst thing we can do is to work at night and sleep during the day. It is totally against the natural flow of energy.

Secondly, the earth orbits the sun every twelve months, and this causes spring, summer, autumn and winter. The sap rises in the spring, creating fresh energy; the summer is a time of fullness and mature growth; fall is the time to harvest and winter is a period of dormancy. All of life follows this cycle, and we are all part of this natural formula. That is why it is best to start a new business in the spring, work hard in the summer, reap the rewards in the fall and plan during the winter.

Many people are not aware of the third cycle. The sun is in motion in the galaxy and completes its own vast cycle every 25,000 to 26,000 years. Because the earth goes around the sun, it is part of this larger orbit. Just as the day is segmented into twelve hours and a year into twelve months, this larger period of time is divided into twelve parts of about 2,100 years each. These energy patterns are relative to the twelve signs of the zodiac, and form the blueprint of the planet earth.

We are now nearing the completion of one of these 2,100-year periods. We are leaving behind what is known as the Piscean Age, and we are moving toward the Aquarian Age. This means that we are going to have a change in energy on the planet ... a change in thinking ... a change in our way of living. Already you may have noticed changes in your own life you cannot explain. One confusing aspect of this change is a speeding up of time. Has time accelerated, or has our perception of it changed? When we know what the changes are, we can adjust our lives to the new vibrations so that we can be more successful. There are certain formulas of success for the next age that are different from the previous age.

Those who study astrology and astronomy are in close agreement that the change started around the turn of the century — close to 1900. When you wake up in the morning you go from dusk to dawn, it is a very confusing time that only lasts a few moments. Because we are dealing with very large numbers, this changeover will take approximately 100 years, completing between 2000 and 2010. As there is confusion with any change, like when I moved from England to America, there is also confusion when the earth moves from one age to another. Change indeed is confusion. It is not unreal to expect confusion for a hundred years. We're nearly at the end of it. Therefore, I'm not disturbed by what's going on. I know it is the necessary cleansing that has to take place before we enter the next age, like the darkness before the dawn.

We need to open ourselves to change. And to understand what we are changing to, it is good to first understand what we are changing from.

Since we are dealing with specific astrological concepts, there are several aspects to understand. For example, each sign of the zodiac has its own symbol: Pisces has the fish; Aries, the ram, etc. Each age also relates to one of the four elements: earth, water, air or fire, and this relationship defines many of its characteristics. In addition, these elements relate to the fourfold nature of man: earth corresponds to the physical; water, the emotional; air, the mental; and fire, the spiritual.

So the flow of each astrological age is determined by its sign of the zodiac, the element of nature and the aspect of man's fourfold nature. For example, the last age, Pisces, revolved around the zodiac symbol fish, the natural element water, and the human nature of emotions.

The astrological age comes first, then the religion of the age. Most recently, Pisces was the age and Christianity was its religion. The symbol for Christianity and Pisces was the fish. The food was fish: If we are good Christians, we eat fish on Friday in remembrance of the crucifixion of Jesus. In the Catholic church, bishops wear a fish's mouth on their heads, called a miter. Who were the followers of Jesus? Fishermen. He could not have chosen anybody else, because it was the Piscean Age.

The Catholic Church realizes this connection, even though it does not teach these principles. Nevertheless, the chair the Pope uses for state occasions has the twelve signs of the zodiac carved on it as does the back of the altar in Canterbury Cathedral in England. The Pope's ring, engraved with a fish, is called the Fisherman's Ring.

Fish come from water, and water is the element of the Piscean Age. What has man's main method of travel been for the past 2,000 years? Primarily by boat. How is a person initiated into Christianity? Baptism with water. And Jesus punctuated his teachings by walking on water, changing water into wine, and stilling the watery storm.

The nature of water is emotion. The Catholic Church and all the churches that come out of Catholicism have been highly emotional. Priests wear vestments, there is incense and the church has stained glass windows. Jesus died for sinners, and if we are going to be good Christians, we have to suffer. This emotional emphasis is the natural energy of Pisces. Fish, water and emotions are natural to Christianity because they are symbols of the age.

Going back another 2,100 years to the previous age, Abraham, the father of the Jewish nation, was born just prior to the year 2000 BC. Abraham had one son, Isaac, whom he was told to sacrifice. Being obedient to the voice of God, he built an altar of stone and was about to kill Isaac when a voice spoke to him from the heavens. Abraham saw a ram caught in the thicket, and he sacrificed the ram instead of his son. At the precise moment in time, the Age of Aries the Ram began.

Just as fish was the food of the Piscean Age Christians, lamb was the food of Aries and Judaism. If you go to a Jewish festival such as the Feast of the Passover, sheep will still be served ritually as part of the menu. But it has nothing to do with diet: It was strictly because of the astrological age. The Jews took rams' horns and used them to make trumpets; they drank from rams' horns; the ram and the sheep became a dominant feature of their lives.

Just as the leaders of the Piscean Age were fishermen, the great teachers of Aries were shepherds. Moses tended the flocks of Jethro for forty years before he became the greatest leader of all Judaism. The great prophets Elijah and Elisha lived in the wilderness with sheep. The king of Israel, David, was a shepherd boy before he became king.

The element of the Age of Aries was fire. Initiation was not by water but by burnt offering. The Old Testament tells us of the pillar of fire leading the Israelites through the desert and Elijah going to heaven in a fiery chariot. God spoke to Moses from a burning bush, not from a puddle of water. Man did not know who he was through his emotions. Fire represents the spirit, and therefore spiritual revelation is discussed in the Old Testament. So the energies of the Age of Aries the Ram were spirit, fire and sheep.

Before Aries was the Egyptian Age of Taurus the Bull. The Egyptians worshiped the bull; they carved bulls on their buildings, and buried the sacred white bulls in crypts. Taurus is an earth sign, which is why Egypt built the pyramids out of earth and rock. In addition, different stone monuments such as Stonehenge were built throughout Europe during this age.

The food of the Egyptians was not fish, not sheep, but beef. A man's wealth was determined by how many cattle he had. The bull was their food, their wealth and their lives.

Each religion builds on the previous one. Everything Jewish came out of Egypt. The laws Moses put forward and his teachings were based on knowledge learned in the Egyptian courts of Pharaoh. Even the word "Israel" was strictly Egyptian (as you will see in Chapter Three).

Then the age changed to Pisces and Jesus presented the Old Testament teachings in higher and refined forms and Christianity evolved. In much the same way, the churches of the coming age are going to be built on Christianity. Christianity as we know it will change. Not that it is wrong; it is just that we have moved into new energy.

As we change ages, there is a tendency to cling to the previous age. For example, when Moses went up the mountain to get the Ten Commandments, his followers became afraid of the impending change. They took all of their gold trinkets, melted them, and made a golden calf, which they worshiped. When Moses came down from the mountain, he was furious! He told the people to grind the golden calf into gold dust, to put it into water and to drink it because they were no longer living in the age of Taurus the bull.

The same types of things happened in Jesus' time. Jesus was Jewish, and because the people still followed the Jewish teaching, it was natural for them to give Jesus titles that come from the Age of Aries the Ram; the Great

Shepherd, the Lamb of God, etc. Actually, it would have been more appropriate to call Jesus the Great Fisherman, the Fish of God. Holding onto the past is the biggest problem we are facing right now as we enter the Age of Aquarius. People want to hold onto teachings of the past.

So what is this coming age all about? The symbol is a man with a water pot pouring water on the earth. The symbol is not an animal, but a man. Physically it is the tending of the planet, ecology. More people are going to become conscious of plants and flowers and trees. Thus we see the emergence of such organizations as Greenpeace and Save the Whales. Teachers of the coming age are not going to be fishermen or shepherds; they are going to be gardeners and caretakers of the planet. We are going to open some of the secrets of the vegetable kingdom, knowledge of which will be of benefit to us all with gardens that flourish with marvelous growing things. We've seen just a glimpse of what lies ahead in the new agriculture from the story of Peter and Eileen Caddy and their Findhorn garden. Physically, people will want to spend more time in nature. Even in cities, trees and flowers will become a priority.

What is the food of the next age? Obviously not fish, sheep or cattle. Vegetables! People are going to become vegetarian for various reasons: health and economic as well as a new soulic consciousness. And this ties into the emotional aspect of the age, which is oneness with nature and animals and plants and all life. When we enter the consciousness that we are one with all life, there is no way we could kill an animal, so there is no way that we could eat one.

Aquarius is an air sign, and consequently we are traveling more and more by air. It is a natural evolvement. in addition, air is the sign of the mind, and everything we know will be learned through the mind. Metaphysically, pouring water on the earth is pouring knowledge. We are in the age of the mind, of learning and having computers to store information. So spiritually, people will be reached through the mind, not emotions. The churches reflecting the energy of this age are Unity School of Christianity, Christian Science and Science of the Mind. They all direct their teachings to the mind. People will learn mentally rather than emotionally. The use of affirmations is one example.

When people learn and reason, they do not want to rely on others to tell them what to do and to make decisions for them. In the previous age, people expected only a chosen few to know and lead. There were kings and emperors and czars and popes who were considered divine. The masses were regarded as sinners and ignorant and did what the leaders told them to do.

As this age dawned, people began to doubt the system. The Russian Revolution overthrew the Czar and revolutionaries shot him and his family. World War I caused the fall of the Kaiser in Germany. The last emperor of China was kept within the walls of the Forbidden City so that he could not see his people in rebellion.

In the United States, there is a great resistance to the president, whoever he is. We do not want one man telling us what to do. Ballot initiatives are taking the legislative powers from the Congress and giving them to the people. We are entering the Age of Aquarius. The whole system of government as we know it is changing. People are going to want to make the decisions for themselves.

In business, organization is going to go from a vertical arrangement, where there is a chairman of the board and then the executives down to the janitor, to the horizontal, where every individual is equally important. Japan was one of the first countries to realize this change. Even in their

American factories, floor and assembly workers wear the same clothes as the executives. And the executives have their desks in the assembly area rather than the upper floors of the building. Instead of the executives telling workers what to do and how to do it, they go to the workers and ask, "How can we do it better?" ... and they listen!

Also the monetary system will change. It is so outmoded and so outdated that is cannot exist much longer. We cannot enter the next age with the system we have, so the quicker it changes, the better. A new monetary system will fit the times. Therefore, we will be better off. It is not bad that it should change; it does not mean we are all going to starve and die; we are just going to create a better system.

When we wake up to the power within, we see ourselves more Godlike. The church has to change its direction and move with the times which is to teach people that the power is within. We can call it the Christ within, the God within or the consciousness within. The terms are totally unimportant. The important thing is the power is within us. We are of God's divinity. We are the microcosm of the macrocosm, and when we wake up to that we will attain and succeed.

Then we will see that we are royal, and it is going to dawn on us that everybody is a king or queen in his or her own right, and we are never going to look at anybody as superior or inferior ever again.

So the coming age is an exciting time. We have the opportunity to bring brotherhood and love and peace on this planet like never before. When we see it as individuals and attain, it will affect the businesses where we work. Then the businesses will catch on, and it will affect the nations and each country will see that it is equally important as the others. It is beginning to happen right now, and we can be a part of it or stand on the sidelines.

But we have to know how to make the transition. The first step is to realize that we each have this energy, power and ability. The second step is to realize that everyone else has it, too. When everyone is aware of having it, there will be peace and there will be love. Finally, we must understand how the changes that are coming are another expression of the world seeking balance. All things in nature seek equilibrium. So, too, this is true in the affairs of men and women who are never truly content unless they are in balance.

As I close this chapter, I return to Peter Caddy and his remarkable wife, Eileen, whose intuitive awareness prove to us that there is direct pathway to the great energy that synchronizes life. Her power of inner awareness also demonstrates that to a greater or lesser extent each of us have intuitive abilities. When we learn to accept as genuine reality that each of us, individually, can, with decision and effort, build a bridge to the cosmic mind by developing our intuitive abilities, then we have made the first step to personal transformation.

All the great thinkers of the world have theorized that intuition works through and with the mind in helping us to glimpse the order, ratio, harmony, pattern, proportion, and musicality of the universe, and both these levels of consciousness seem indispensable to this task.

It was Rene Weber, professor of philosophy at Rutgers University, whose statement about human possibilities is a fitting way to conclude this chapter: "[It was] Albert Einstein who said that contemplating the grandeur and the laws of the universe was so awesome that its only proper response is the mystical response. Reflecting on the strange parallelism that enables mankind actually to have glimpses into cosmic patterns and organization, Einstein said that 'the most incomprehensible thing about the universe is that it is comprehensible.'

"Now one might ask: how can an appreciation of the great universals of religion, philosophy, and science transform the personality? My answer is that, viewed with utilitarian eyes and in an Archimedean attitude, it cannot do so. But neither can the mere reading of a text on mysticism turn us into mystics or dissolve our minds. All these are only catalysts, preparing the way. Therefore, I end on the note [that] there must be an active harmonization. Ordinary daily mind must become the instrument for cosmic mind, and that is itself the transformation of the personality. No further step is needed, because that is the turning about in the deepest seat of our consciousness, the movement at the spot that can integrate our lives."

Finally, we must learn to accept that those powers (such as intuition and clairvoyance) which seem the strangest to us are the most natural and common, and if we but allow ourselves, they are the bridge builders to the universe.

Chapter Three

Creativity

*Let love move through your life to be a light
to the world.*

Alexander Everett

In the last chapter I explained the power of balance to
you. I told you the story of Peter and Eileen Caddy and how
this couple demonstrated the balance of the outgoing male
love quality with the female attribute of intuitive wisdom.
This third chapter will define your natural genius and how
to apply it in a fashion that is creative. Think of the Caddys
and their interdependence when I tell you that your number
one power is the understanding and practical use of
oneness. Your number two power is awareness of the
separate parts of oneness, the male and female attributes.
Your third power, which I will explain in this chapter,
comes from the combining of the male and female attributes
— two components to obtain a third part. The obvious and

most creative combination of male and female is in the conception of a child. The newly born baby is the result of the union between of two complementary energies. From two comes three. So you now have three separate entities, man, woman and child. Three individuals that make up a family of oneness.

This concept of three in one, one in three, all separate parts yet all in one, is found throughout religion. For example, the Christian religion has revealed through the teaching of the Trinity the idea of three in one, all three parts separate, yet inseparable as being one. Designated the Father, the Son, and the Holy Spirit, the Trinity is somewhat male oriented. It omits "mother," replacing that reference with "Holy Spirit" or "Holy Ghost." Yet the mystery remains of how three separate parts could, at the same time, be regarded as one.

The Jewish teachings, likewise, touch on this three-in-one concept. Abraham, the father of Judaism, had a son, Isaac, who had a son, Jacob, who had twelve sons who multiplied to become twelve tribes. Jacob then said, My name is no longer Jacob, but my new name is Israel. This word Israel consists of three syllables, IS, RA and EL. Much of the Jewish teachings and heritage came out of Egypt. Even Moses, the great leader of the Jews, lived in Egypt during the first forty years of his life. The etymology of the word, Israel, shows that the first syllable, IS, comes from Isis, the mother god of Egypt. EL is the male, masculine force as found in the first syllable of words such as Almighty, Elohim God and Allah. RA is the name of the god of light in Egypt, which is the result of the interaction of the IS and EL. RA, the light, is the same as the child — that which is created. Thus, another way of saying father, mother and son is to say Love, Life and Light. The father is the masculine, standing for love. The mother is the female, standing for wisdom, the life force. When it is combined with the male energy the creation of a child or son occurs, like a great light. So let love move through your life to be a light to the world.

The symbol, the three-sided equilateral triangle, represents the three aspects of creativity, which are all equally important, namely the Father, Mother and Son which represent Love, Life and Light.

This information comes from very ancient knowledge which may help you understand your own great latent power of creativity. This concept of the Trinity, the Triad, the Law of Creativity has, throughout the ages, permeated the religions of the world. With the explanations developed in this chapter, you can take this knowledge and use it effectively in your life.

Most people, however, are unaware of their latent genius that lies like a sleeping giant inside them. They know that an Albert Einstein or a Michelangelo were geniuses, but to accept that they, themselves are geniuses seems improbable. We have been trained to ignore the stirrings of genius within ourselves, that the only difference between you and Einstein or Michelangelo is that they developed and used their natural genius ability. Your genius remains dormant.

Now let me explain how the concept of the trio, father, mother and child, or love, life and light — all three of which exist within you — can help you define who you are and what you should do with your life.

First of all consider the male part of you. The love that you give out in the form of your work, your job, your vocation, your career, that which you make available to others and share with the world. Next, combine the love you give out, your maleness, with your female intuition to give you direction, how and where to perform your creative work and service. Then the child of your combining — the light — will shine for all to see, as you slowly, but surely, develop your natural genius ability. In other words, you will discover that you, as well as everybody else, are a natural born creator.

I'm going to tell you a children's story (We all are children at heart, aren't we?) that illustrates the genius ability in each of us, and how so often we try to substitute who we really are for an idea that we should be somebody else. This story will help you recognize that you don't need to be anything but what you are. The story is about a stonemason. This man lived in Japan at the base of Mount Fuji. All he had was three possessions: a small wheelbarrow, a hammer and a chisel. Being a stonemason, he cut little pieces off the bottom of Mount Fuji and carved them into pagodas, put them in his wheelbarrow and set them up in people's gardens. That was his job, that was his way of life. He was a stonemason.

But one day he created the most beautiful pagoda he'd ever made, and he took it to the emperor's palace and he placed the pagoda in the garden. As he was doing this, the emperor drove by in his carriage. The stonemason looked at the emperor, and said: "Oh, he's so powerful, he's so wise, he has so many talents and abilities. I wish I were the emperor."

He wished so hard that he actually became the emperor. (I did tell you it was a children's story!) Then he drove out in his carriage. "Now I'm the emperor. I shall be able to tell everybody what to do. I'm more powerful than being a little stonemason." And he had fun being the emperor.

But, do you know what happened one day? He was out riding and the sun played down upon his head. He looked up in the sky, and said, "Sun, please cool off. I am the emperor, and I'm the most powerful."

Guess what? The sun didn't obey. The emperor said, "Oh. If the sun doesn't obey me, the sun must be more powerful than I am. I wish to be the most powerful. I wish I were the sun." And he wished so hard, he became the sun. And then he could shine on everybody, and some people would get more sunlight than others, because he made that decision, because he was the most powerful. He really had fun playing being the sun.

But do you know what? One day he was shining and thinking what fun it was, when some clouds came along and got in the way. He couldn't shine on people. He said, "Now wait a minute. I'm the sun. I'm the most powerful." But the clouds stayed in the way. He suddenly realized that the clouds were more powerful than he was. And he said, "Oh. I wish I were the clouds."

And he wished so hard that he became the clouds. Now, he thought, "I'm the clouds. I can rain on some people and not on others." He had fun doing that because he controlled everything. He was the most powerful: Nobody can live without rain water.

Then one day, something happened. He was blowing along as a cloud, and he hit the side of Mount Fuji. He blew on it; he rained on it. But it didn't move. And he said, "I want that mountain to get out of the way. I'm the most powerful." But the mountain refused to budge.

So he said, "Wait a minute. That mountain must be more powerful than I am if it doesn't move." Obviously, he wished to be the most powerful. So what did he wish to be? Mount Fuji. He wished so hard to be Mount Fuji that he became Mount Fuji.

Now he really had it together. The emperor worshiped him, came down and bowed before him. People did the same thing.The wind blew on him, the sun shone on him, and no one could move or disturb him. He was having so much fun, because at last he was that great person he always wanted to be: He was Mount Fuji.

But guess what? One day, he heard a funny little noise at his feet. He looked down and what did he see? He saw a little man with a hammer and chisel cutting him up into little pieces that he was wheeling away in a wheelbarrow. He said, "Wow! I'm not the most powerful. That man can cut me up into little pieces and wheel me away. He's obviously more powerful that I am."

Since he wished to be the most powerful, he wished to be the stonemason. And he wished so hard that he became the stonemason.

The moral of this little story is don't wish to be someone else. It's okay to be who you are. Just as the stonemason was the stonemason, to be anything else is foolish. You have a natural ability, a personal power and gift that nobody else has but you, so don't ever, ever wish to be anything or anybody else.

Now that you've read the simple story of the stonemason, I want to quote from a more serious source, Ravi Ravindra, who wrote piercingly about the haunting question of "Who am I?"

"Who am I? Am I Judas, am I Jesus? Out of fear, out of desire, I betray myself. I am who I am not. I cover my face with many masks, and even become the masks. I am too busy performing who I think I am to know who I really am. I am afraid: I may be nothing other than what I appear to be; there may be no face behind the mask. I decorate and protect my mask, preferring a fanciful something over a real nothing.

"I cling to the herd for comfort. Together we weave varied garments to cover our nakedness. We guard the secret of our nothingness with anxious agility lest we should be discovered."

I say to you, don't be afraid to be discovered. Don't shrink from finding the light that will illuminate who you are. I am going to help you find out what your personal creative contribution is in life. Before I do this, I need to point out to you that whatever work you choose to do, or service you wish to render to others, it must always be for the good of others. See yourself and what you do as a way of giving assistance to others in blending your love and life to give forth light. Unfortunately, there are many people who are always looking for personal gain. These are the frightened souls Ravi Ravindra writes about. They work for money and use it as a false measure of their success.

Never work for money. Remember to make your first priority the desire to direct your energy to help others. When you do this, automatically you will receive sufficient rewards to meet your own needs. To put it more simply, "Do what you have to do and the money will follow." I would also add, "Your life works in direct proportion to how much you help others in the work that you do."

Now, we've arrived at the crucial question: What are you going to do with your life? How do you find the genius within and put it to work for you and others?

The answer to that important question occupies the next few pages, and they may be the most important words you've ever read. I'd like to start the exploration for the genius within you with another story, which I think you'll find intriguing:

Long, long ago, the Greek gods lived on Mount Olympus. This sacred place was the home of the gods. According to history and tradition, these gods created the world. They brought not only the world into being, but also created man.

They decided it would be good to make man in their own image, to be powerful like they were. The question arose as to where they would place this power. If they made it too easy for man to find, man might rise up against them and overthrow them, and they wouldn't want that to happen!

So, they discussed amongst themselves, "Where are we going to place man's power so that he won't find it too easily?" They all had incredible ideas. One god said, "Let's place it in a cave and put a big boulder outside so he can't get in." Another said, "Well, if he's as ingenious as we are, he'll have no difficulty in rolling the stone back and finding this power within the cave. I don't think that will work."

Another god said, "I've got a great idea! Let's place it on top of the highest mountain in the world. He'll never get up there!" Then he said, "Wait a minute. If we're going to give him the same power as we have, surely he will find it there. I don't think that's too smart."

They kept on thinking of ideas of where to place the power of man. They thought maybe under the ocean. Down there it would be hard to find. Maybe deep in a forest far away from where anybody has ever been. However, nobody found the answer that seemed to fit.

Then one god came up with a brilliant idea. He said, "I've thought of the place that man will never think to look!" They all asked, "Where's that?" He said, "The answer is very, very simple. The answer is to place the power of man right inside him. He'll never, ever look there!"

Well, is that not true? Most of us spend all of our time in life looking around elsewhere to find power and energy. The last place we look is right inside ourselves!

So how are we going to find our personal genius quality? This natural ability that we have?

As I may have observed before, there are three basic ways to discover this. The *first* is to go back in time to when you were about twelve years of age. That is the time in life when we all have desires and fantasies about what we want to be in life. But when you have told someone, a parent or teacher, he or she may have said, "Don't be silly! You don't have the brains to do that!" or "There's no money in that. I don't think that's a very good idea!" And so your wonderful dreams and visions were crushed. It is very sad.

When I was twelve or so, as I wrote earlier, I had a vision, I had my dreams and ideas about being a teacher. I remember telling my parents how I wanted to be a teacher, and my mother said, "Alexander, I wouldn't do that if I were you! I don't think that is what you should do in life!" She did her very best to persuade me to do something else.

Luckily for me, I persevered with what I wanted to do. I overrode my mother's suggestions, ideas and visions about my future. So I say to you, go back, and see what you wanted to do when you were young. You have a vision buried deep within you. Maybe it has been covered up; maybe it has been mislaid; but it can be recovered. So that is my first suggestion: See what your natural ability is by looking back to when you were a child about twelve years of age.

The *second* way to discover your genius is through the centering process which is described in Chapter Ten. The knowledge of our life's purpose is stored in the center of our being. We can ask: "What is my genius quality?" "What is my natural ability?" "What job should I do in life?" When we are still enough, all is revealed. But do not be surprised at how the answer comes: It may be a flash of light, but more often it is a subtle knowing in the form of intuition.

The *third* method is called the "rainbow technique." Every one of us is born under the influence of one of the seven colors of the rainbow. Just like our astrological sign, we cannot change it. We are blessed with a talent or an area in which our genius lives, and this energy pattern vibrates in tune with one of these seven colors more than the other six. The entire human race can be divided into these seven clear-cut classifications according to their individual traits.

Another thing to consider is the color next to your primary ray, as these traits might be slightly integrated. In astrology, it is termed being on the cusp. For example, if you are a red, you might also have a little orange. But you would never have red mixed with violet, because these colors are at completely opposite ends of the rainbow.

But beware! Sometimes the thing that is the strongest in us can also be the most destructive, so the negative as well as the positive is described. But do not be upset. Once the negativity is identified, it can be turned around and made positive.

(By the way, this rainbow process has nothing to do with what color clothing supposedly suits you best.)

The following story of the scorpion illustrates what can happen if you misuse your genius.

There was a little scorpion who wanted to cross the river. He couldn't swim, but he saw a big, old, fat turtle sitting by the edge of the water. He went to the turtle and said: "May I sit on your back so that I can get a lift across the river?"

The turtle said, "No way!"

The scorpion asked, "Why not?"

The turtle answered, "I know how you are. You'll sting me. I don't want to die! So I'm not going to let you get on my back. Forget it."

The scorpion said, "Now look, I want to get across the river. Why would I sting you? I'll drown, too!" and he finally persuaded the turtle to give him a lift.

So the scorpion got on the back of the turtle. The turtle started swimming across the river, and, halfway across, the scorpion leaned forward and stung the turtle on the back of his neck. The turtle started to drown. With his last gasp he said, "What did you do that for?"

The scorpion answered, "It is just my nature!"

When we misuse our gift, it becomes our sting. We are like the scorpion, so be careful how you use your talents.

Following is a description of the primary colors of the rainbow and how each one is related to a strong aspect of character in a human. Further information concerning the colors of the rainbow will be given in Chapter Ten.

Red = Physical = Leader

Red is the physical color. If you belong to this group on the red ray, your characteristics are that you are very physically courageous, very forceful, active, energetic, fearless and have a great deal of will power. You like to tell people what to do. You are a natural-born leader.

This great strength can also be your sting. You can misuse your leadership qualities and over-control. You may have the tendency to be obstinate. No leader likes to be told what to do. You may also be a little proud. But if you use your qualities in a positive way, you will be a great leader.

What kind of job should you seek? You need to be in a position to tell other people what to do. You would be a good boss of a company, or a manager of a department or business, the owner of a corporation or perhaps the chairman of the board. If you are born with the qualities of the red ray, you are never going to be happy unless you have the opportunity of telling others what to do.

Orange = Emotional = Risk-Taker

The next color on the rainbow is the color orange, the emotional color — the color of feeling. If you are born on this orange ray, you will be a person whose life is influenced by emotions. You are one of the people who speculate and take risks in life. You do not think much, and are not very practical; you *feel* everything. You are affectionate, kind, generous, very sympathetic. You love people and want to share with others. For example, if a person goes out with an orange person, the orange person will buy drinks, pay for the meal and tend to go first class.

On the downside, orange people let their feelings run away with them. They become too loving and over-generous. The are literally the up-and-down type people: switching and changing. That is your nature if you are an orange person.

In the business world, you also have your ups and downs. Your feelings will lead you to be successful if you speculate. You tend to make a lot of money, but often lose it. Not to worry! You will speculate another day, and be successful once more.

There are many areas where orange people can excel. Real estate sales, a business of speculation, is right up your street. You buy land, divide it up into lots, sell it and make a fortune. Or, there again, it might not work out, and you end up a loser. That is what speculators do. You make good salespeople. you get excited about things; you are kind and want to help people. You are good at marketing, promoting, you would make an excellent entrepreneur. You would enjoy multi-level organizations, or wherever the skills of salesmanship are needed.

Yellow = Mental = Thinker

Yellow throughout history of man has always represented the power of mind, wisdom and knowledge. Yellow represents the thinkers of the world. Your characteristics are that you are very philosophical in your outlook on life, you are full of ideals, you like to have principles of a high standard, you are a great dreamer. However, since your head is in the clouds, you often remain spaced out and somehow forget to come down to earth and put your concepts and ideals into action. You the thinker tend to remain in the realm of the mind, oblivious to the practical aspects of life.

On the negative side, because you are somewhere out there, you are often inaccurate, absent-minded, very unlikely to be on time; you probably isolate yourself and live in a world of your own making.

What do you do in life if you belong to this yellow-type thinking group? Since you think and philosophize, you tend to be creative more than most people. You are inventive, your thinking is very analytical. You are the idea-type person. In the business world, there is one glorious place to put people who are on the yellow thinking level — the research and development department. You make a great contribution in life: you design new products, you are the innovator, and above all you have a wonderful creative power. If these remarks fit you, you will know that you are on the yellow ray.

Green = Balanced = Business Person

Green is the central color of the rainbow, the most balanced color. People on the green ray have the power of being in balance. Your chief characteristics are as follows: You are a very together person, you have a great deal of common sense, you are down to earth, you are a very practical person, you are accurate. You are result-oriented, you work well with figures and numbers, you like the books to be in order: the debits and credits must balance. These are your greatest assets.

But they become your negative traits when carried to extreme. For example, if someone who works for you makes a mistake, you fire them on the spot. You can be very unforgiving, hard and narrow in your thinking. So, if you are green, you are project-oriented, not people-oriented. You are so concerned with numerical results, you overlook the feelings of other people. Experience, however, can temper your judgmental tendencies.

It is pretty obvious where green people should be in the workplace: bankers, accountants, bookkeepers, statisticians, record keepers or financiers. Any job that concerns money and figures where results are more important than people. Nevertheless, green people are great, industrious workers whose contributions give an organization fluidity and success.

Blue = Love = Teacher

The color of blue is the color of love. If you are born on the blue ray, your natural tendency is to be loving and kind, and to be very desirous of helping other people. That is why teacher is the key word for blue, for what is the greatest way to help another person but to teach him how to become effective and successful in life? Your main characteristics are that you are a very aware and intuitive person, you take everything that happens in life very calmly, you have the power of endurance, you are patient, you are always speaking words of love and encouragement. You enjoy raising the consciousness of another person.

It is hard to believe that blue people could have a negative side to their personality. They do. One obvious negative trait of a teacher is they will bore you with all of their detailed explanations about everything. Another negative aspect is that they play the part of knowing it all. Because they feel they know it all, they can be cold and indifferent.

What kind of jobs best suit a teacher? Obviously, a school teacher; however, there are many other areas where you as a teacher can work. In the church, you can become a priest or minister and be the one who explains and teaches all about religion. In sports, you could be an instructor and coach on the field of play or in the gymnasium. Or if you serve in the military, you could become the sergeant major who drills the troops and explains to the enlisted men what to do. In the business field, you would probably end up being the personnel manager.

Purple = Gifted = Artist, Healer

Purple, sometimes called indigo, is the next color in sequence. The color purple is associated with people who are born with a natural gift and are capable of working well in the field of the various arts and crafts. Your characteristics are as follows: you are a very self-reliant person, you are strong and determined in what you should do in life, you have your own style and way of doing things, you are very clear about how you want to live. This applies in the way you dress, which is usually unconventional and different from the average person. Because you are strong and self-reliant, your negative characteristics tend toward making you opinionated and perhaps too set in your ways. Also, because you are good at what you do, you tend to criticize and judge others for their shortcomings.

What do you do in life? Well, according to the specific form your talent takes, you could be any of the following: a singer, dancer, actor, painter, sculptor, writer or poet. Included in this group are healers: doctors, surgeons, dentists, chiropractors and massage therapists. What you do, you do naturally. Of course, you might need some training to better your skills, but if you do not have the natural ability in the first place, you will not be successful.

In the business world, it seems that singers and dancers do not have a place. However, in every business there is what is known as a department of special projects. What are these special projects? You would be a person in advertising, photography or magazine layouts. In fact, you could do some technical job that nobody else wants to do but you.

Violet = Centered = Saint

The seventh and final color is right at the center of the rainbow. This is the color violet. The two key words are saintly and supportive. If you are violet, your main characteristics are that you are a very centered and together person, you are loyal to people with whom you work, you are very loving, devoted, kind type of people. You are truly a saint, a saint delighting in assisting other folks, putting out a hand to help other people.

What in the world could ever be negative about being a warm, loving, faithful, supportive person? There are a couple of weaknesses. If you are one of these saints, you do not like working alone. You always need somebody else to work for or with, you just cannot make it on your own in life. You also cannot abide another saint coming along and doing your work for you.

I made a big mistake years ago when I was in business. I had a secretary who was a saint. Secretaries are usually saints. She'd do anything for me. And did. Great lady!

But eventually the business got big, so we employed, unknown to us, another saint. We had two saints sitting at two desks next to each other. They spent their entire day tearing each other's hair out. They cannot abide anybody doing their thing. It's *their* thing. If you have one saint, don't, for goodness sakes, employ another one!

In some extreme cases, if you are truly a saint, you will allow people to walk all over you and become a doormat. You like to suffer a bit, like all good saints do.

What kind of jobs do these people do? Well, you make good secretaries, nurses, waiters and waitresses; you could be a clerk in an office or a shop assistant. You can be in any job where you are supporting another person or organization.

Color Combinations that Work

If you want to have a good marriage or partnership, certain colors relate to each other better than others. Usually, opposites seem to get along best, because the colors complement each other. The strengths balance out the weaknesses.

For instance, red leaders love to marry saints. Saints like to have somebody to tell them what to do. It makes a wonderful combination. But the man doesn't have to be red. There are many red ladies in the world, and they should always seek husbands who are violet.

Another pair that gets on very well is yellow and green. Yellow's idealist head is in the clouds while green's balanced feet are on the ground. What yellow creates, green will manifest.

Blue teachers love purple people, because they love to teach and talk about purple's talent. That makes purple people happy, because their talent is given to the world.

There is one color that is left over: orange. Oranges only get along with oranges. A wonderful marriage is two oranges, because they gamble with each other, they argue with each other, they cheat on each other and have a ball doing it! They both play the same game, so they understand the rules and have fun at it. That's their nature!

There are certainly many of us who are unsure about our gifts and our life's work. But I've discovered that most people do know what they should do, but are simply not prepared to see what it is. If you are one of those people who prefers to remain ignorant of your ability and don't want to know what you should do in life, it may be because you don't want to face the responsibility for yourself and for performing some hard work. Me, take responsibility for myself? Forget that! Of course, eventually every one of us must face who we are, or live a life of frustration and unhappiness. There is an exercise for any person, reluctant or not, to figure out what his genius is.

Here's how it works: Take a clean sheet of paper and write down all the things that you enjoy doing. List all the pleasurable experiences you have had. Put down anything that comes to your mind which you enjoy doing. Make the list as long as you like; take time, don't hurry. Use more than one sheet of paper if needed. Look at your list carefully, go over each item one by one and gradually cross out those ideas that don't appeal as much as when you first wrote them down. Take your time, at least a day, maybe longer, reviewing your list, progressively eliminating some of your original thoughts until the list is shortened to three or four ideas, but no more than seven.

Then use the "sleep technique," to determine which possibility is really the answer. (See Chapter Eight for a description of the sleep technique.) Find out what happens when you wake up in the morning. You may discover that the answer that comes to you is something you enjoy doing and may have been just a hobby. But you can't visualize yourself doing your hobby for a living. You feel you couldn't make money doing that. Of course, this is not true, many people have converted their hobbies into a great sense of satisfaction, with property and cash as tangible rewards.

A man, some years ago, who was a dentist, used to attend my seminars and he frequently told me how he disliked being a dentist.

So I asked, "Why did you study and train to be a dentist if you didn't like it?"

He answered, "Because my father was a dentist and I figured out that being like him was a good way to make a living."

Then I asked him, "What do you really enjoy doing?"

He said, "I love playing the trumpet."

So I replied, "Then why don't you become a trumpet player?"

The answer came back, "Because there is no money in playing the trumpet."

Well, to cut a long story short, I persuaded him to take up trumpet playing in his spare time. This he did and joined a small amateur band on the weekends. He so enjoyed doing this, that one thing led to another and one day a week, on his day off, he started taking trumpet lessons. He joined a larger, more professional band and made more money. His enjoyment increased as he became a better trumpet player. I eventually suggested that he leave off being a dentist and become a full-time musician.

He said, "I can't afford to do that since I have a family to support and can't make enough money working in a band."

It took me more than a year to persuade him to make the change. Well, eventually he took the plunge and finally became a full-time professional trumpet player. Some months later, I met his wife on the street and I asked her how everything worked out.

She replied, "It is just great, my husband, the ex-dentist, is happier than I have ever seen him before in his whole life, all because he is doing what really makes him happy. There are no more family squabbles. He is relaxed and has fun with the children. There is no more tension or stress. We are all getting along so well together that we are now a completely happy and united family."

I asked her how matters were working out financially.

She replied, "I am not really sure whether he is earning as much as he used to as a dentist, but who cares? We are all having a wonderful time together and that's what really matters."

Finally, she added that he had sold his dental practice, and with the money they had bought a new house, fully paid off. So here was a good example of one man turning his hobby into a profitable way of living.

You may hold to the idea that money is hard to make. In reality, it is mainly a matter of doing a job that you enjoy. You always achieve more when you are excited about what you are doing. It is that simple. Now suppose that what you want to do doesn't work because you lack the necessary knowledge and skills. The answer can be found in your female side, your intuition. Take time out, cat nap, listen to your inner voice guiding you to the source of the information you need. All the knowledge you require already exists. It is all a matter of tuning into your female intuitive side to find out what you need to know. Unfortunately, many of us limit ourselves, because we have bought the idea that we are not gifted or capable enough, or don't deserve to be successful. The truth is, you are a creative person with your own natural genius ability. All you need to do is to accept that everything is possible, and follow the principles of creativity as presented in this chapter, understand how they work and put them to use right here and now.

In the end, finding out what your genius is involves asking yourself deep questions about who you are and where you fit into the grand scheme of things. I was impressed by the statement of Marty Kaplan, a former speech writer for Vice President Walter Mondale, whose confession of discovery appeared in *Time* magazine:

"Some people manage to find purpose ... making from wholly earthly values a sufficient basis for moral choice and a meaningful life. Love — even if it can be reduced to psychological explanations — can still make the world go round. Justice — even if its origin is political — can still be legitimate. Beauty — even if its perception is hostage to the taste of local tribes — can still move the spirit.

"That is where I thought I would spend my life: a cultural Jew, an agnostic, a closet nihilist.

"Of course I didn't like it. Who wants to face death without God? Who wants to tell kids that the universe is indifferent to them? But the alternative — faith — was unavailable to me. Once the mind thinks some thoughts, it cannot unthink them.

"What attracted me to meditation was its apparent religious neutrality. You don't have to believe in anything; all you have to do is do it. I had worried that reaping its benefits would require some faith I could only fake, but I was happy to learn that ninety percent of meditation was about showing up.

"The spirituality of it ambushed me. Unwittingly, I was engaging in a practice that has been at the heart of religious mysticism for millenniums. To separate twenty minutes from the day with silence and intention is to worship, whether you call it that or not. To be awakened to the miracle of existence — to experience Being not only in roses and sunsets but right now, as something not out there but in here — this is the road less traveled, the path of the pilgrim, the quest.

"The God I have found is common to Moses and Muhammad, to Buddha and Jesus. It is known to every mystic tradition. In mine, it is the Tetragrammaton, the Name so holy that those who know it dare not say it. It is what the cabala calls Ayin, Nothingness, No-Thingness. It is Spirit, Being, the All.

"I used to think of psychic phenomena as New Age flim-flam. I used to think of reincarnation as a myth. I used to think the soul was a metaphor. Now I know there is a God — my God, in here, demanding not faith but experience, an inexhaustible wonder at the richness of this very moment. Now I know there is a consciousness that transcends science, a consciousness toward which our species is sputteringly evolving, a welcome development spurred ironically by our generational rendezvous with mortality."

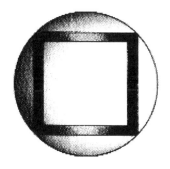

Chapter
Four

Fourfold Nature
of Man

*Still the physical, emotional and mental to
become aware of the spiritual.*

Anonymous

In this chapter, I wish to show how you function in four distinct and identifiable ways, how your mind can be used as the instrument that, in its holistic manifestation, can link you up with intuition, and can help you orient yourself more effectively in your journey toward understanding the wider dimensions of universal consciousness.

As a person, you function in four distinct ways, and in a very precise sequence. First of all, there is your physical body, with all its different limbs and organs, flesh, muscles, bones, blood and skin. This is the basic you at the outer physical level, and it responds and reacts to your feelings and your sensitivity, which represent your emotions, your second level of consciousness. In turn, emotion is controlled by your third body, your mind and thinking process. Each of these three states works interdependently and in conjunction with the other two levels of consciousness. What you do at the physical level is affected by your emotions which are controlled by your thoughts.

It so happens that all these three bodies are dual by nature — they perform in a negative or a positive mode. It is you who decides whether to have good or bad thoughts, which bring you pleasant or nasty feelings, which, of course, determine how you perform physically, whether beneficially or harmfully.

There is a well known saying that describes what I have just said, "As a man thinks, so does he become." Positive thoughts create loving feelings and bring about good actions. Negative thoughts create harmful feelings and result in bad actions. This is very true and it seems that everybody knows and understands this fact. The big question is, what makes a person think in a positive or negative fashion in the first place?

Many years ago, when I first started teaching seminars to adults, I thought, in my ignorance, that I could teach people how to think in a positive manner, so they would feel good and change their lives. My work at this time was called Mind Dynamics. I was referred to as "the father of the human potential movement," in recognition of my work to help people use the latent power of their minds to improve their lives and to reach out to the source of limitless understanding.

I set out to explain how the mind functions, how to engage its power and to apply the power beneficially. Alas, when my students returned to their homes, their enthusiasm for Mind Dynamics wore off and they fell back into their old habits and ways of thinking.

There were a few who did benefit. They applied what I taught and discovered remarkable results. The excitement lasted for this small group, which represented about ten percent of each class. I called these successful students the ten percenters and eventually made an interesting discovery. It happened when I was was flying from San Francisco to London. Sitting next to me was the chief executive of the European division of a large American corporation. We got to talking and I told him that I taught seminars on how to use the mind in a positive manner. He listened, then told me some of his experiences dealing with top management, men who represented his company in the major European countries.

He extracted a large binder from his briefcase and revealed the pictures, personal history, education and records concerning the contribution of each of the men in his company. He had a complete dossier on each executive. He then made a statement that I never forgot: "Ten percent of my people make a good profit for the company. Eighty percent just get by. They are reasonable people, but business-wise, they only just about break even. The remaining ten percent, I wish the opposition would hire!"

I was shocked at his sincerity. I found it hard to believe what I heard. He was kind enough to offer me a job for the rest of my life if I would teach a larger percentage of his executives to join the ranks of the ten percent who made handsome profits for his company. Regretfully, I declined, because, unfortunately, my results in teaching also showed only ten percent success. On my return to the United States, I made inquiries into other large business establishments and, much to my surprise, the ten percent rule seemed to apply everywhere.

Through continued study and observation, I came to the conclusion that only ten percent of any group of people think in a positive manner and obtain successful results in life.

I also observed that newspapers thrive on printing stories about accidents and disasters, death and destruction. They feed on the readers' negative approach to life. Television and radio operate with a similar negative mode. No wonder ninety percent of us look on the down side of things and only ten percent stay positive in their behavior.

Realizing that I was on the wrong track teaching mind power alone, I let Mind Dynamics go and for almost a year I stopped teaching. During this interlude in my life, I spent much of my time alone. I was living in San Francisco, adjacent to Golden Gate Park and near the ocean. I started to run on a daily basis on a circuit through the park, treading on the jogging and bike trails. For a change of scenery, when the tide was out I ran on the sands toward the zoo and back, or to the seal rocks. The daily routine cleared my mind and landscaping my garden also freshened my brain cells. I built a small rockery and goldfish pond complete with fountain. I sat in my bay window, looking at the flowers and listening to the falling waters of the fountain as I relaxed with classical music in the background.

During that year of 1974, I came upon a great realization. It became the turning point in my life. I discovered that the mind is not the source of power, of expanded consciousness. I discovered there is a vast, limitless power beyond the mind, a fourth state, of which I was only vaguely aware. Up to this point in my life, with my experience of being a school teacher and the founder of three independent private schools, as well as the creator of Mind Dynamics, it had been clear to me that the mind and intellect ruled supreme. Now, I became aware of the fourth state of consciousness which is the *source* from which everything you do evolves.

It is the higher, inner *self,* the *soul* of man, the *spirit* which lies at the center of every human being.

If you like, you may wish to call this your God center, that point from which everything emanates. Now, this energy, this power, this higher intelligence, being of God is perfect. God does not make mistakes. This fourth body level is the key to success. Unlock the door to this inner realm and you open yourself up to the flow of the power of God, which is perfect.

Remember, as I mentioned earlier, the first three body levels, physical, emotional and mental are all dual by nature. They, all three, can be used in both a negative and positive way. However, this fourth body state is not dual by nature, it is single in its perfection, being of God. God is good, always right, and does not make mistakes. So, now you have the answer. If you can become aware of the fourth state of consciousness, you will find the perfect influence on your creation of positive thoughts. In turn, this influence will bring good feelings to your emotional state, which finally creates right and proper actions at your physical body level. Of course, the trick is how to find and activate the God source, the spiritual body state of consciousness.

To give one answer to this perennial question, I've called on Dr. Renée Weber, professor of philosophy at Rutgers University and the author of many articles on comparative East–West philosophy. Referring to the bridge humans must build to create a link with the universal mind, Weber uses the word Harmony:

"Now I will briefly sketch some of the specific ways in which this harmony can be brought about. There is, first of all, meditation. Meditation is one of the great harmonizers. It synchronizes all the aspects of ourselves and creates the bridge between the light and the seeming darkness. Second, there is visualization, which is used in all traditions. There are examples in the Yoga Sutras of Patanjali, of visualizing role models. In Buddhism, it is identifying oneself with the perfect ones, with the *Dhyani Buddhas.* It isn't a mere imagining or fantasizing — those words are too weak and sound like thought playing a game with itself — but it is visualization, which is an energy and a force, and therefore does something in the world. We would say, in theosophical language, that it means building thought forms. Thought forms are recurrent patterns of energy which hold, as it were, the record of our aspirations, our feelings, our personalities, our fears — our *everything.* Thought forms can, as we know, be negative or they can be healing. Repeatedly building these transparent structures of very real energy, thought forms can help the active mind via intent and resolve, to link itself up with its deeper and ordered energies and to build patterns which will become allies in the transformation of the personality. This is used in healing, and in healing the mind — though *it* is not the healer — can help prepare the way for the universal healing energy to come through. Therefore, the mind is in this instance again an active agent for transformation."

The mind as an active agent for transformation. What a marvelous thought Weber brings to us! And he reminds us that preparation for transformation, for linking up with the fourth state of consciousness, is facilitated by our awareness of some steadfast spiritual principles embodied within the Seven Laws or States of being. If you understand and follow them, you will have taken a long step toward linking up with the fourth state of consciousness and your life is bound to be successful.

The symbol for the fourfold nature of man, physical, emotional, mental and spiritual is a square, where each side represents one of the four bodies of a human being. The sides of a square are equal in length. Likewise, it is significant to realize that the four bodies of man are equally important. The spiritual fourth state of consciousness might appear to be of the greatest value, but not so, because without the mind, the emotions, and the physical body, the spirit within you would have no place to manifest results. All four bodies are of equal value. To increase the significance of the square as a symbol, consider the four directions of the compass, in which each side of the square faces North, South, East or West. These are four coordinates of the compass.

West: This direction represents your lowest level, your physical body. There is a saying, "Go west, young man to make your fortune." The implication of going west indicates going in the direction of making money, having material possessions, being financially independent and becoming physically wealthy, which would include having a healthy physical body.

South: This direction represents your emotional body. Consider geography for a moment; if you are on the continent of North America and you go to the north to Canada, it becomes colder; if you go south to Mexico, the temperature rises and it gets warmer. The people who live in the south exhibit more feeling. They run their lives by their emotions. In the south, there is more compassion and more love. Likewise, it is here in your emotional body level that you express your own personal feelings and the desire of love. There is more warmth here than in other parts of your consciousness.

North: This direction represents your mental body. Geographically, it is colder in the north. Your mind is cold and logical in its intellectual thinking process. Your mind plans and thinks in a very precise manner. Consider the map of Europe; I was born in England, in the north of Europe, where I was taught to develop a cold type of rational thinking, never to show my emotions and feelings. To shed a tear of compassion or to cry openly was frowned on. I was taught to keep a stiff upper lip.

However, in the south of Europe, in a country like Italy, the emotions ran riot and people operated from their feelings. Italians, by and large, feel, whereas the English mainly think. When you consider what happens to countries south of the equator, the reverse takes place. The northern attributes become the domain of the south and vice versa, because here, when you go north, you are nearer the equator where it is warmer.

East: This direction represents your spiritual body. You look to the east to grow spiritually. Years ago, all the great cathedrals and churches in Europe were built with their altars facing east. So, generally when the congregation is facing the altar, the people are looking toward the east and praying to God, as if God dwelt physically in the east. In the Bible, it says when Christ was born, a star appeared in the east, and that wise men followed the star to Bethlehem, where it stood still so that the wise men could find and worship the Christ and become more spiritual. Likewise, the Muslims in the United States, when they pray, face Mecca, their spiritual center, which is in the east.

The Native Americans have a similar symbol. Their elders and shamans teach the wisdom of the "medicine wheel." This symbol is literally as old as the hills and is based on the four directions — north, south, east, west. Wild animals are chosen for their characteristics, which stand for the qualities found in the four different points of the compass. West is represented by the physical power of the black bear. Darkness come from the west when the sun sets and most black and dark thunderstorms bring their power from the west. The bear itself is a great symbol of physical power.

South is the place of the heart and sensitivity, and is depicted by the deer, a gentle, docile, and loving animal. North is the direction of the mind. Here is found an animal that thinks and calculates. It is the wild wolf, which displays a cunning mind and a great memory. East is represented by the noble eagle, and is the spiritual direction. When bad weather arises, the eagle is the only bird known to fly high above the storm. Likewise, when you are functioning at the spiritual dimension, you can fly and rise above the storms of life. Remember, the eagle is one of the symbols of the United States.

This knowledge of the fourfold nature of man is profound. It is expressed in the geometrical form of a square, in the four points of the compass and in the Native American medicine wheel. It is written in the stars, it is part of planet Earth, and it is found in your own personal four body levels.

Now you should know how to activate these four body states. Everything in life works from the inside out. For example, in order to perform a mundane, physical act as simple as driving a car, you must first learn to use the controls, to perform the actual art of driving. Likewise, to be a creative, successful genius you have to know how to use your fourth state of consciousness. This special inner state is the place from which ideas and genius-creating energy emerge. Everything you do starts with an idea; no idea, no action. The word idea comes from the Latin word *Dea* which means a goddess. In other words, ideas are brought into being by using your female God power, which is none other than the intuition.

The method of awakening this sleeping goddess within you is to get into an appropriate state for this to happen. There are certain conditions that must be met before ideas will flow from your fourth state of consciousness. First of all, you must relax your physical body. Also, it is helpful to keep your body fit with sufficient exercise to oxygenate the blood. Walking is very calming and relaxing. If you get upset, take a long walk and you will be surprised how much better you will feel afterward, especially if the walk brings you in close contact with nature, in particular flowers and trees. Never underestimate how the power of nature will bring peacefulness to you.

In concluding this chapter, I have called on John Algeo, professor of English and head of the department at the University of Georgia, to give us his viewpoint on the process of the connection of the individual through the mind, with the fourth state of consciousness:

"Let us not forget, however, that all of our intellectual accomplishments rest upon a severe limitation in how we perceive the world around us. As Hamlet says, 'There are more things in heaven and earth, Horatio, than are dreamt of in your philosophy.' There are riches in heaven and earth that are not and that cannot be dreamt of in any philosophy of the human mind.

"So when *The Voice of the Silence* says that the mind is the great slayer of the Real, this is the slaying it refers to — a necessary limitation on our perception of the Real, necessary for our stage of evolution. But when we come to the next stage of evolution, the stage to which the Path leads, we must go beyond the limitation of the mind to perceive Reality in a more direct and fuller way. And so *The Voice of the Silence* goes on, 'Let the disciple slay the slayer.' The mind in its turn needs to be slain — that is, limited in the way *it* limits our awareness of Reality. When the mind is slain, we do not lose the benefits of the mind — we only free ourselves from *its* limitation. To slay the mind is to know Reality more fully, to drop the veil, to take off the mask and let our original face appear.

"How does one slay the mind? Who does the slaying? Here is the positive role of the mind in the transformation of the personality. The mind slays itself. And it does so by becoming still. The process of meditation is the stilling of the mind, the slaying of the slayer. When the mind ceases its constant chatter and becomes very quiet, we perceive another sound — the Voice of the Silence. The Voice does not come into existence only when we fall silent and start to listen to it. It is there all along. Just as the original face is ever behind the veil but appears only when the veil is removed, so the Voice of the Silence speaks eternally but is heard only when we become quiet enough to listen. It carries on a conversation with us that has no beginning and no ending — but is continuous. It is the Self talking to our selves. To hear the Voice, to become aware of our ongoing conversation with it, we must be still in our minds. More particularly, the mind must still itself."

Chapter Five

Five Senses

Your senses are the five gateways to knowledge.

Expansion of your senses is important because a broader appreciation of life around you will sharpen your mental processes and hone your ability to act effectively in decisions you must make.

Pretend it is early in the summer and you decide to visit your favorite place in the country. As you look around, you observe the distant landscape and the vegetation nearby. You hear with your ears the birds singing, the bees buzzing and a gentle breeze whistling in the branches of the trees. You smell with your nose the scent of the wild flowers, the tree blossoms and the aroma in the atmosphere. The serene beauty that surrounds you may even leave a flavor on your tongue. You are touched by the experience of being in nature as you feel through your skin the warmth of the sun's rays on your face. You are alive to signs and signals of nature through your five physical senses of seeing, hearing, smelling, tasting, and touching. With them you can witness and enjoy everything that exists in your favorite place in nature.

Let's examine now how your five senses can lead you to learn from nature.

The power of nature is probably the largest influence on this planet. If you communicate with nature, it will change your life. By being in nature, by observing its qualities, you can learn powerful lessons.

Take, for example, a flower you might discover in your favorite nature place. A flower is a perfect manifestation of God. As an exercise on how you compare with this perfection, there are ten characteristics to consider. If you score yourself from one to ten (the flower always scores ten), the exercise will give you a strong indication of where you may need to improve your life. To learn from the flower, you must be honest with yourself and score accurately.

1. A flower is always centered.

A flower is so centered, it makes everything with which it comes in contact feel better. It attracts people. That's why we give flowers to the sick. When you are in the presence of other people, do you irritate them and upset and frustrate them, or are you, like a flower, so centered everyone loves to be in your presence?

2. A flower is always beautiful.

You never see an ugly flower. It does not matter what the color, you can even mix them all together, they are always beautiful. Human beings often have frowns on their faces, and their beingness can be unattractive by the way they express themselves. Whatever is inside you is going to shine through your beingness. Do you reflect outwardly your inner beauty?

3. A flower always smells nice.

It has a beautiful fragrance. Some people have bad breath and body odor. Why? Because they eat meat. That is one reason for offensive odor. By and large, if you are vegetarian, you will not give off a bad odor.

4. A flower cannot speak, but if it could speak only three words,it would say, "I love you."

A flower does not care whether you love it back; it just smiles at the universe with an expression of devotion. When you wake up in the morning, what do you say to the first person you meet?

5. A flower is fourfold in its nature the way people are.

It lives on sunshine and fresh air and water, which it draws up through its roots; also it draws minerals out of the earth. Human beings should have the same priorities: sunlight first, fresh air second, pure water third, and the elements that come out of the soil, number four.

Where do we get our minerals? From the soil as well. In the book of Genesis it says man should live by the fruits and grains of the earth. When we eat the "fruits," we do not destroy that from which the food comes. If we eat grain, we do not eat the grass. If we eat a grape, we do not eat the vine. If we eat apples, we do not eat the tree.

One of the major things I hold to is that I am not here to teach you to be vegetarian. I am here to teach you some principles, which if you understand them, you will be led to do what is right.

Let me put it this way. I know many people who are into hatha yoga. Now you can practice standing on your head and may never become enlightened. However, if you do become enlightened, you might find the value of hatha yoga and want to stand on your head.

If you comprehend spiritually who you are, then you will be led to eat and exercise correctly and not take in harmful substances such as tobacco and alcohol, and eliminate unbalanced behavior.

6. A flower has physical strength.

Flowers grow from seeds and are so determined to grow they can break through concrete. Within that seed there is everything necessary for it to become whatever it is supposed to be.

People also come from seeds. You also have everything within you that you need to become what you are supposed to be. But when things get tough, when life is difficult and jobs are scarce or whatever it is, we look for somebody else to do it for us. Flowers cannot get food stamps, welfare or a free handout; they have to do it for themselves. They are so determined to be flowers that nothing will get in their way.

Once, in San Francisco, I planted some geraniums on the wrong side of a fence that was six feet high. Geraniums usually grow about three feet. These grew six feet so that they could look over the fence and get the sunlight. They were so determined to flower, they went the extra three feet.

How about you? Are you prepared to work hard so that you can flower?

7. A flower is a perfect example.

A flower could sit on a chair and say, "Follow me because I'm beautiful, I'm centered, I'm loving. I am perfect."

In all honesty, I cannot sit on a chair and say to you, "Follow me because I have it together." I have much that might be helpful, but I cannot say that I am a perfect example. None of us really is. But the flower can make the claim of perfection.

8. A flower does its work happily.

It does not say, "My flower union says that unless I get the basic wage I'm not going to flower today." Many of us do not go out and create our own genius because we are afraid we are not going to receive what we think is necessary. So we do not flower. We want to get the cash up front or have a written agreement. It never occurs to us that, if we flower, the world will give us what we need.

My point is that whenever you go out for the right reasons and do it, you'll be amazed at your reward. And every time you go out with, "How much money am I going to make? Blah, blah, blah," then you limit yourself. In fact, you'll get even less. It is the way things work.

You know, you are part of the universe and as you give of yourself, the universe supports you. But some of you never dare do that. I know that's your problem. I know people all over the world who are frightened to give the universe their beingness. It is tragic.

9. A flower never makes a mistake.

The flower is so at one with God, it has no ability to choose not to be. It automatically does the right things.

Because we are human, we have the ability to choose. The only reason we are sick, the only reason we do not have good relationships, the only reason we do not have the right job, the only reason all these things do not work in our lives is because we choose them. We are greedy. If we can become like the flower, at one with God, we will never make a wrong choice.

You see, if you so become one with God, you become God-like. And God doesn't make mistakes. It's only when you separate yourself from God that you make mistakes; of course, your intellect is so smart that it thinks it knows all the answers. When the spirit makes the decisions, it can only make the right one. Because the spirit is one with God.

10. A flower likes being the flower it is.

A rose does not wish to be a daisy; a daisy does not want to be a geranium. Each one of us has abilities that are unique to us. When we discover what our unique qualities are and act on them, then we will be happy. That is all a flower does — the best it can be being what it is.

We're all uniquely different, and we all have the ability to truly flower, and truly be ourselves. But, do you know what most of us do? We play a game. We say, "Oh, I wish I were like so and so, because I'm sure he's got lots more ability than I. I'm just nobody." (Remember the story of the stonemason?)

Your five physical senses are the five avenues through which you become aware of your surroundings. It may seem obvious, but your five senses are also the gateways to all the knowledge that you will ever learn. You see and read books, articles and newspapers, You see and watch television. You listen to lectures and conversations. You hear people speak on the telephone, radio and television. Your five senses are literally the openings and channels through which your awareness operates. All knowledge that you learn in a lifetime you become aware of through the use of your five senses.

In recent years, there has been talk concerning an extra sense, a sixth sense. What is meant by this sixth sense? It is a way of referring to a collective sense beyond the five physical senses. This extra, sixth sense is the sum total of all the other fifteen senses, which go beyond the basic five physical senses, and lumps the fifteen together and calls them the sixth sense. It is another way of saying something very similar.

Years ago, you never used the term "sixth sense." At that time you never considered moving much beyond your physical and emotional body levels. Only a few people were aware that each of the five senses can function at the higher mental and spiritual levels. Today, more and more people are recovering the ability to function at all four body levels as pertains to their five senses. I use the word recover, since I have come to realize that you and I are not evolving to become greater and more aware persons, but we are returning, going back, to regain, to recover what we were once able to do.

This is a time of renaissance, or rebirth, of reawakening, of becoming aware of your full potential. Everything already exists, and is already known. It is just that you have been asleep to the fact that you have many senses, instead of just the five that you were taught at school. You are entering the age of going within, becoming peaceful, stilling the mind and becoming aware of a storehouse of knowledge that lies deep within you.

I have been a teacher all my life and when I taught in England, I always used the same address to new students. I would say: "My job as a teacher is simply to help you discover what already exists within you so you may reference this knowledge and use it in your daily life. Because I am an educator and teacher, it is my task to bring out of you what you already know. I even go further and say that many of you have greater ability and talents than I do and will achieve far more in life than I ever will."

My young students were very attentive and anxious to learn from a teacher who, instead of telling them what to do, created a climate and atmosphere in the classroom in which they could grow and expand according to their individual gifts and talents.

What I said to those students all those years ago, I say to you who are reading this book. Many of you will do greater things than I and that is wonderful. So read these words and draw upon the great storehouse of knowledge that lies within you.

How does each of the five senses I described in the introduction of this chapter function at four different levels of consciousness? I will start with sight, the ability to see with your eyes. Look at a picture hanging on a wall. If you gaze at this picture objectively, you will see a colorful, oblong shaped object whose purpose is to appeal to your sight. Many of us view paintings as a decoration that covers an empty space. We don't go beyond our physical vision level of awareness.

Next, look at this same picture from an emotional standpoint. When you do this you will discover that you have a definite feeling about the painting. You will discover that you are attracted or repelled by the painting. What you feel about it would be a very personal response. According to your own tastes and desires the painting would touch you in different ways emotionally.

Next, look at this painting mentally. Use your mind to intellectually understand the painting. As you do this, you will notice the style in which it was created. Maybe you can discern what school of painting the artist comes from. Is the painting classical, modern or abstract? Is it composed in oils or water colors? Has the medium of charcoal or crayons been used? You could generate a continual flow of thoughts regarding the painting.

Finally, look at the painting spiritually. This is when you may discover that there is a deep and profound meaning in the artist's message. It is an extension of himself. Many artists become frustrated because they hope to present to you and the world their own unique talents. There is a direct connection between the artist and his painting which, being a creative expression, becomes one of the artist's children.

As a school master in England after World War II, I frequently went to Spain for a vacation. One of my favorite haunts was Toledo, the old capital city of Spain, with its narrow streets and magnificent cathedral. In the sixteenth century, the famous artist El Greco did much of his painting in Toledo. He was born in Greece, but for many years worked in Spain, so he was called "El Greco" which means "the Greek." His paintings had a dual aspect, subjective and spiritual, yet physical. Frequently, he would paint a miniature scene in the corner of a large canvas. I identify with this artist because my work has been based on the interaction of the two realms, spiritual and physical. Although El Greco lived four hundred years ago, I know I would have liked him if we had met because I feel I understand the message he portrays in his paintings. In fact, when I lived in Fort Worth, Texas, years after I became enchanted with El Greco in Spain, I was driven to a private home, on Christmas Day, of all days, to view a private collection of valuable paintings. The room was large and I exclaimed as I walked in, "Oh, there is an El Greco on the far wall."

My hostess was amazed. She said, "Yes it is an El Greco, but how did you know from such a distance?"

I then explained my feelings about and understanding of El Greco's work. Today, you can visit the Kimball Art Gallery in Fort Worth where this particular El Greco is now part of a permanent exhibit.

Next, consider one of the other senses, in particular, hearing. Just as you can see a picture at four different levels, you also can hear, with your ears, what a person is saying at four different levels. Suppose you attend a lecture. You will physically hear what the lecturer is saying. Your ear drums will reverberate with the sound of the speaker's voice. You literally will be hearing physically. If you were to attend one of my lectures or seminars, you would find that I have a very strong and powerful voice. So much so that you won't be able to go to sleep, even if you sit in the back row. I guarantee you will hear me physically and I will make sure that I keep you physically awake!

Next, you can hear me emotionally. You will be aware of the intonation of my voice and, as I project excitement and urgency into what I am saying, you will start to get a feeling of what the words really mean. The more fervor that I project into my speech, the more enthusiastic you will become about what I am saying. Remember, in order to make a sale, you have to move the customer emotionally. This, of course, includes the way you put feeling into your voice. If you speak in a warm and loving manner, you gain more attention from whomever you may be conversing with. In order to get people to really hear you emotionally, you need to be excited, to be enthusiastic, to be outgoing and to be outrageously yourself.

Next, you can hear mentally. It is simple to be aware if you are listening mentally. When you hear someone make statements that seem important to you, what do you do? You make a note of what you heard, you write it down on a piece of paper. That means you heard it intellectually. Mentally it made sense to you. Your mind wants to store this knowledge. The writing down process reinforces your memory. Because you spent many years in school, your mind has been trained to hear well at the mental body level. The last time I heard someone lecture publicly, the talk lasted about one hour. I can well remember the way the speaker was physically dressed and the power of his physical voice. I can still feel his enthusiasm and how his lecture moved me emotionally. However, at the mental level, the written notes that I made were only three sentences on the back of an old envelope. Mentally, I received very little from this hour long dissertation. You may be shocked to discover how little of what you hear mentally is retained, or even remembered. There is a well known saying, "What you are speaks so loudly, I don't hear what you are saying." The physical and emotional presentation will influence you more than the words actually uttered. This is the usual course of events.

How do you know when you hear something spiritually? The fact is you frequently hear spiritually without realizing what is taking place. It works something like this. You hear a statement in the form of words which you don't understand logically, yet somehow these words seem to make sense. In fact, deep down inside, you are aware that what was said was absolutely right, but you have no means of verifying it, but at the same time you know inwardly that what you just heard is correct. A conflict takes place between the outer mental, logical and intellectual thinking in contrast to the spiritual level which does not have to make sense. Yet you know what you heard is true and accurate. What actually took place is that the spoken words that fell upon your ears woke you up suddenly to what you already knew. The words uncovered and revealed an area of consciousness that had lain dormant for a long time. The fact is, there is nothing new in the world. Everything has already existed. It is just a matter of waking up and discovering what is already known. To hear spiritually is the highest level at which you can hear. It is the ultimate step that you need to take, because if you hear spiritually, you enter the final phase of hearing, when you know that you know.

You may not yet have cultivated the ability to hear spiritually. To tune into spiritual hearing, it is good to take time out and practice becoming quiet and peaceful. Direct your attention to the innermost part of your being. Continue to remain in a peaceful, tranquil state. Feel what it is like to be still and centered. Be aware of this state of consciousness. Then, the next time you need to hear words spiritually, create the same sense of quietness and peaceful receptivity and you will then discover you can hear inwardly and spiritually.

Thus, the four ways that you can hear what is being said are: first of all, to physically hear the vibrations of the words being spoken. Second, you can hear emotionally as you pick up the feelings that the speaker is projecting vocally. Third, you can hear mentally as you write down what seems important to you intellectually. Fourth and finally, you can hear what is being said spiritually when, in silence, you wake up to the fact that you already know what is being said. You literally know that you know.

I have now covered two of your senses, namely seeing and hearing. What about the other three — smelling, tasting and touching? These three senses are less developed in human beings, but more developed in animals. Each sense has a different range of operation. Seeing is the most powerful and has the greatest range. You can see for a longer distance than you can hear. You can hear for a greater distance than you can smell. You can smell farther than you can taste. And touching comes at the end of the line. The five senses are on a descending scale from the most powerful, seeing, down through hearing, smelling, tasting, to the least effective sense, touching. All the five senses can be used at four different body levels, but I have only demonstrated seeing and hearing because they are the two senses you rely on the most. The other three, smelling tasting and touching are only used physically except on very rare occasions.

Seeing and hearing are more acute in the animal kingdom. A predator bird, such as a hawk, can soar and float several hundred feet above the ground, see a tiny mouse below in the grass, swoop down, pick up the mouse in a flash and enjoy a mid-morning snack. However, as I gaze out of my window at the fir trees in the distance, I can neither see the fir cones or the birds on the branches. An owl can see in the dark, but I have to depend on a flashlight. My miniature donkeys prick up their ears at a sound in the distance that I never hear. Animals' ability to smell is even more amazing. I take my two golden retriever dogs on a daily walk around a little lake at the back of my property. The two dogs walk, nearly all the time, with their noses glued to the ground, picking up all different kinds of smells. Then suddenly, they detect the scent of a deer and they are off to the races, following the trail, but all to no avail, the deer have long gone.

I have often wondered what would happen if a person's sense of smell became as developed as that of a dog. Just imagine if you could follow the trail of another person by picking up the scent of her perfume, shoes and clothes. That would be hilarious, but why not? This was well portrayed in a jocular sense, in the film *The Scent of a Woman*. Al Pacino played the part of a blind man. Having lost the sense of sight, he developed his sense of smell and was able to follow the scent of a particular woman whom he desired. If animals can use their sense of smell to follow a trail, maybe you could learn to do likewise. It seems that in some ways, animals are more sensitive and more aware than human beings. The place where I live is called "Animal Paradise." Here, I breed a variety of exotic animals. They are all very friendly because I treat them with kindness and affection. The wallabies eat with the deer. The deer lick the cats. The donkeys rub shoulders with the llama. The golden retrievers love everybody.

There used to be a wild cat that would roam on my property and come by and eat the leftovers I threw into the compost heap. This wild cat never came too close, it kept its distance and ran away every time it saw me coming. Then one day, I heard a loud meow outside. I opened my front door and this wild cat limped into my home. The cat sat on the floor, looked up at me with pathetic eyes, and uttered many terrible, loud meows like I had never heard before. I picked up the cat and discovered it had a broken back leg, a damaged tail and its jaw was all twisted so that it couldn't eat or drink. It had obviously been hit by a car. This poor, wild cat, that had always run away from me, was badly hurt and came to me as a last resort for help and comfort. Unfortunately, there was nothing I could do and I reluctantly put it out of its misery by putting it to sleep. This wild cat had always relied upon its senses for physical survival, but when necessary, it was able to call upon an inner sense to help it survive. The cat knew inwardly that I was one who cared for animals. The cat tuned its senses into a deep spiritual level where anyone who tunes into the fourth body level feels and senses the inner power of togetherness and oneness. It is the land where everybody speaks the same language. The lesson I learned from this unfortunate experience with the wild cat was that when any person or animal tunes into a deeper level of consciousness, he or she will enter the arena of oneness. Here, everyone realizes he or she is one in all aspects of life. I marvel at animals, who, although they are considered less intelligent than us human beings, are more aware since they use their five senses to such a high degree.

Your five senses are the means through which you can gain access to this storehouse of knowledge. They are literally your gateways and doors which, when open and operative, make available to you all information and knowledge through your ability to see, hear, smell, taste and touch. The more open your five senses become, the more you get to know.

How can you upgrade any one of your senses to a higher level? Think about the blind person whose hearing improves remarkably to compensate for his loss of sight. As one sense shuts down, another becomes more highly developed. Now, consider your sense of hearing. If you only hear physically, you are unlikely to open up your inner ear and hear spiritually. That's why, if you depend on hearing everything at a mental, intellectual level and play the game of evaluating and reasoning, you will never know anything intuitively at the spiritual level. You have to leave behind the lower lever in order to enter the deeper and higher level of your senses. If you are quiet and still, you can enter a higher sensory level.

The symbol for your fifth power that gives you access to your Five Gateways to Knowledge is the five-pointed star. The five tips or spikes of the star stand for your five senses. They point in an outward direction like antennas probing into space to pick up all the knowledge and wisdom that has always been out there throughout eternity. Likewise, when your five senses become sharpened and more spiritually directed, so will your awareness of the miracles of the universe become more comprehensive, bringing to you sounds and signs of the Everlasting which will confirm your own status as a child of God.

As you read each chapter in this book, you should be more able to access your intuitive spirituality. A change will take place for you. You will advance from a lower level of thinking of your self as *Homo sapiens,* wise man *(Homo* is the latin word for man and *sapiens* means wise), to the higher level of *Homo noeticus. Noeticus* in Latin means to know. You will become the person who knows. For when your senses are fully opened you will realize that you know you know, like *Homo noeticus.* This is the ultimate experience of having all your five senses, your five gateways, wide open and operating at the inner, deepest level possible so that, inevitably, you will come to know all that is worth knowing.

Chapter
Six

Work

Actions speak louder than words.

Anonymous

In an earlier chapter I explored with you "finding the genius within." I presented the idea that each one of us has a particular work to do in life and to be happy, fulfilled and prosperous we must find what it is. I suggested that one method to discover the genius within you, the work that will grab your imagination and passion, is to remember what vocation or practice captivated you when you were about twelve years old, or older.

If you go back in your mind, chances are you will identify the inspiration that compelled you when young — the idea that swept you away in a dream of building bridges, or teaching children or tinkering with automobile engines. The description of the work doesn't matter, your dedication to it does.

Such dedication to action is one of your greatest personal powers. Unfortunately, the idea of work has been misapplied. Why? Because most people look upon work as toil and drudgery. We view work as something we have to do during the week to make enough money so that we can have pleasure and a good time on the weekend.

Work becomes a different conception if you are doing what you enjoy doing. It becomes pleasure, an activity that wholly absorbs the individual. Since this is the case, why not choose a job that gives you the opportunity to do what you most like to do? Actions don't have to be dull and dreary. Actions can be fun and enjoyable. To which you might reply, "I have to take a job that pays well. If I don't earn a reasonable salary, I won't be able to pay my bills."

This is the mistake in reasoning that most people make and need to avoid. They place money first and job satisfaction second.

If you are one of these persons, you need to reverse the order of your priorities. If you don't enjoy performing your job, no amount of money will make up for your loss of enjoyment and happiness. You will become stressed, miserable, and the quality of your life will suffer. Sickness and illness may occur. The extra money you may make at an inappropriate job may be used up to pay the bills you create because you are living a strained life instead of one that is joyful because you are doing what you enjoy.

One example of popular thinking about the meaning of a job in a person's life was demonstrated to me one Friday evening when I was preparing to give a talk in a hotel prior to the start of a weekend seminar. I walked into the men's washroom and there was a young man smiling and whistling a tune as he combed his hair in front of a mirror. I said, "You seem very happy tonight."

"Oh yes," he replied, "it is Friday night, my work week is over and now I can enjoy myself and get drunk."

My immediate reaction to this youth's statement was one of disappointment. Then after a few moments of reflection, I realized that his attitude reflected what is typical of many people who work Monday through Friday to earn enough money to celebrate their release from labor on the weekend.

I saw another example of the division of work and pleasure in people's minds just recently. It was Monday morning and a utility company was drilling a hole under the road across the street from my property to insert a pipe so that phone lines could be threaded through it under the road. I made an observation about the progress of the work, and the foreman said, "Oh well, it's Monday morning and we always work slowly on Mondays since we are still recovering from the weekend." On reflection he added, "On Fridays we also slow down in preparation for the weekend."

I thought, isn't it marvelous to create an arrangement where one only works effectively for three days of the week. This attitude seems to be too often prevalent in the work place.

I have always liked the following saying, "Happiness is a means of traveling and not a station to arrive at." This is definitely true. You can be happy every moment of the day as you travel through life doing what you delight in doing. There is no need to think that you have to work hard and long hours all your life so that one day you can retire and enjoy the fruits of your labor in your old age. In other words, don't think of happiness as the station you arrive at when you retire. This is not true. You can be happy throughout your whole life year by year as you practice your skills in an area of work that you enjoy performing. In fact, this so called station in life that you arrive at when you retire is not always the wonderful place of happiness you had hoped it would be. Because if you do retire and stop working, something unexpected takes place. At the exact moment you quit working, your batteries start running down and you move in the direction of dying.

There is a wonderful commercial on television that advertises a certain brand of batteries. A rabbit keeps on beating a drum as he keeps on moving along while around him others let their less efficient batteries run down as they become casualties along the road of life. The secret to the rabbit's long life is that he keeps on moving and beating his drums, realizing he has a powerful battery to keep him going. You, likewise, have a powerful battery, and as long as you exercise your personal power of action and keep on beating your drum to the rhythm of life, you will live longer than you could ever imagine.

It should be emphasized that active working is living and not working is dying. The actuaries, those people in the insurance business who calculate the risks involved in living and dying, will tell you that figures show that the average person does not live for much longer than five years after he retires and quits working. All life insurance policies are based on life and death statistics; that's how insurance companies make their money. So the chances are that at whatever age you retire, you won't reap the financial benefits of an annuity or a pension for more than five years. To avoid being a statistic, you need to do something you enjoy doing and that keeps you young, so you can keep on going and going and going. The secret to a happy, long life is to keep working happily in your field of endeavor. However, if you do retire, immediately take up another interest in life, at which you can happily engage and keep on going and going and going. Remember, "Working is living and not working is dying."

I have a small orchard of apple trees at my home and I have made a simple observation concerning apples. Apples are either green and growing or when they become ripe they quickly rot. As I liken myself to an apple, I prefer to be green and growing as I happily work at what I do. I don't want to retire and become ripe and start quickly to rot and fall apart. I pick my apples in my orchard every fall and many of them I place on shelves in a specially built apple shed. If I don't eat them within a few weeks, the rot sets in and I have to throw them onto the compost heap. I personally don't want to retire and sit on a shelf and gradually rot away. I much prefer to remain green and growing. I would never say I am going to live to a "ripe old age." However, I might say that I am going to continue to be green and growing. In fact, as you grow older, the more you realize how little you know. The need and urgency to work, to do, to achieve, to be active, if anything, becomes greater. For, as you grow older, the more clearly you perceive how little you know and how much more needs to be accomplished. This is certainly true in my case. As the years go by, I see an even greater need to impart what I have learned in life so that other people, like you the reader, can learn how to have more happy, successful and prosperous lives. My reasoning is — if I can do it, so can you, provided you know how. The motivation that urged me to write this book is quite simple. I want you to enjoy life as I am enjoying life. At the time of writing this book, I am seventy-six years old, going on seventy-seven. I have so much more to do in life that I plan to live for many, many more years to come. I never plan to retire because I want to continue to remain green and growing. Everything that is recorded in this book, I have experienced in my own personal life. I will never suggest that you do something unless I have field tested it in my own life and, in particular, this is one hundred percent true concerning what I say about work and happiness.

The concept of releasing the special energy inside you into work applies to any vocation or job you may decide to do. For example, you might be into sales. You could be selling real estate, insurance, stocks and bonds, cars, retail or wholesale, it doesn't matter what you sell, it is just that you need to express yourself in the art of selling. Once a salesperson always a salesperson. Selling is your interest in your life, it is what makes you happy. On the other hand, you might be a natural born builder, you want to design and construct factories, barns, houses and furniture. You could work with materials ranging from wood, stone, brick, iron to glass. The medium with which you work is not what is important, it is your desire to shape, mold, build, construct and bring into being lasting and permanent construction. Yet again, you might be artistic, which could lead to painting, drawing, pottery, stained glass, weaving and creating all kinds of artifacts. Again, you may be born with the desire to share with the world your inner feelings about life; you have a message to give which could be expressed in one of many forms such as singing, dancing, theater, films and writing. You need to express your desire in the form of action. Action is a great personal attribute and power that you have. Action is the objective outcome of your innermost subjective desires. Yes, "Happiness is doing what you have to do in life."

As long as you keep expressing your desires in the form of work, you will remain happy. So how do you deal with retirement? I certainly know a great deal about retirement, because I am of an age at which most people retire. I am over seventy years old and according to our society, I was supposed to retire at sixty-five or as some people do, at sixty years of age. Well, obviously I haven't, because if I had retired, I would not be writing this book and still teaching seminars in different parts of the world. Since I have come to realize that to work is to live and not working leads to death, I have decided to go on working. I personally enjoy both working and my teaching and also I can't even conceive of the time when I would quit teaching. In fact, as the years go by, the demand for my services seems to increase.

You might say that's all well and good for you, and those who work on an independent basis, but I work for a firm that has compulsory retirement at a certain age, so what should I do? Once your job has been terminated, you immediately get involved in something that interests you, such as a hobby and start applying your ability and place your energy and interest into this other venture. Place your entire mind, body and soul into this new undertaking. Because I personally intend to live to a great age, I have collected articles about people who live to over 100 years old. These centenarians all have one thing in common. They develop an interest that they can work on for the rest of their lives. My answer is very direct, "Don't retire from work unless you want to retire from the human race." Action is a great word. Work is a great word. Happiness is a great word. Retirement is a word to avoid.

It is important to know how happiness comes about. In my own life, I realize that I have always been happy, relaxed and free of stress because I have always done what I enjoy doing the most, which is to teach. This teaching has taken different forms, but I have always remained a teacher. Early on in my life, I coached sports such as cricket at a school in England. I always remember I had the great honor of helping to coach a young boy in cricket who went on to make history and be the youngest cricketer ever to represent England in a Test Match. I also coached tennis and soccer. I continued with my interest in soccer when I came to the United States. To this day, I have a plaque and trophy in my bedroom, that were given to me for coaching Fort Worth United in both 1967 and 1968 to become the undefeated Junior Texas State soccer champions. This proved to me that I could adapt my desire to explain and teach in different forms whether it be in the classroom, at seminars, the lecture hall or in a variety of sports. The question of whether it would be hard or easy to teach never entered my head. I just had to get out there and give what was inside me.

Why is the sixth personal power concerned with the words "action" and "work"? It is no accident. The number six breathes and expresses work in action. God created the earth in six days and on the seventh day God rested. There are seven days to a week and on the seventh day, Sunday, you rest, which implies that you should work for the other six days. However, you know how that goes. Most people only work five days a week and most people would prefer a four or four-and-a-half day work week. Why does this happen? Simply because people, by and large, aren't happy with what they do, so they seek more leisure time in order to avoid what they dislike. If people would choose a job because it suits their skills and not select their occupation based on financial reasons, they would be much happier.

It is interesting to observe that different religions designate the seventh day of rest to fall on different days of the week. If you are a Christian, Sunday becomes your day of rest. If you are Jewish, Saturday is your holy day. If you follow the

Islamic faith, then Friday is your sacred day. Because I often teach seminars on the weekends and travel back home on Mondays, Tuesday becomes my day of rest. Tuesday is the day that I recharge my batteries so that I can go to work for another six days. Six days has always been associated with work. The first miracle that Jesus performed at the beginning of his three year ministry was to change six jars of water into wine. The number six showed that he was ready to actively do his work of giving his teaching to the world.

The symbol for your sixth personal power of action is the Star of David which is also the symbol for Judaism. This Star of David has six points. It is made up of two triangles. The first triangle rests on its base with one point facing in an upwards direction. The second triangle is turned upside down and placed over the first triangle, thus creating a six pointed star. The first equilateral triangle represents your personal creative power (discussed in Chapter Three) at the inner, subjective level. The second equilateral triangle represents creating at the outer, objective level, manifesting material results in the physical world. This symbol is very ancient; it comes out of Egypt and was used by the teachers of the ancient wisdom prior to the founding of Judaism. The Star of David is a universal symbol. The Jews used this symbol to represent their teachings and way of life. However, you or anyone else can use this symbol with understanding when you realize what it represents. It stands for work, your personal power of action, what you do and bring into being by your own personal, active effort. Whatever the inner creative part of you desires, so will the manifestation take place in the realm of the physical through the use of work in action.

Work is the elixir of life. As I have grown older, I realize that what I accomplish through my work in life is the only activity that is important to me. My work is the vehicle through which I express and share myself with other people. It is my work that gives me the most satisfaction. My work is an expression of my heart's desire and the actions that I perform make me happy. Now you can do the same, when you follow the dictates of your heart. If, up to this point in your life, you have been concerned more with making money than enjoying what you do, I would say to you, "You haven't lived yet; you are only existing." Regrettably, too many people are eking out an existence. Why not reexamine your situation, look within and follow your innermost feelings? Find out what you should do, which is no more than your natural ability to work in a field of your own choice. Dare to choose to be yourself. Take a job where you will be actively fulfilled. Fulfillment and happiness lead to success and prosperity. Don't go through life doing something you don't enjoy. Wake up, take hold of yourself, it's your life, do what you yearn to do. Find out what turns you on. Seek an outlet for your skills and talents. If you don't do it for yourself, nobody will do it for you. Go for it, don't delay. I have never heard of anybody regretting being happy, and happy you will be if you do what inwardly you are led to do. So take time out. Sit still and be quiet. Stop thinking nineteen to the dozen, just let go and listen to the inner small voice, your intuition, and get in touch with the inspiration — the work idea — that excited you when you were young. Just discover what it is that you need to do for the rest of your life.

When you transform the genius within into a passion for the work you were born to do, when you can give of yourself, not necessarily your money, but share your talents and gifts with others in a spirit of sharing, then you are truly living, not just existing. You need to make yourself available to life unconditionally by using your skills in your work to create products and services that are of value to others. Then you will really become aware of your personal power of action, which is no more or less than sharing yourself, the best way you can, with other people.

Take your desire, your passion, and with fervor give of your best. Then as surely as the chrysalis turns into a beautiful butterfly, so will your passions turn into profits. The way it works is simple: Whatever you put out in life, in direct proportion you will receive in return. All the great teachers throughout the ages have said, it is blessed to give and when you give of yourself, so will you receive. The saying that I like the best was spoken by Lao Tse, a great Chinese teacher who wrote the Tao Teh Ching. He said, "Give and you will find you already have." Take your deep desires and passions and make them available to the world and you will automatically have your profits. The trick is to do what your heart dictates, and the profits will materialize. So go out into the world and turn your passions into profits.

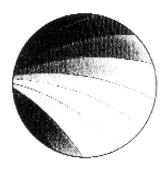

Chapter
Seven

Completion

God rested on the seventh day from all his works, which he had made.

Genesis 5:2

When I was headmaster of my own school in England, I called into my study a boy aged about eleven who was failing in all his scholastic studies. When the apprehensive youngster was seated, I asked him a simple question, "What do you like and enjoy doing most in life?"

His worried expression changed into a wide smile. "I love music," he said.

So I asked him if he would like to learn to play the piano.

His answer was unequivocal. "I have always wanted to play the piano, but my parents said no, because private lessons would be expensive."

I then told him that for the next twelve weeks he did not have to attend any of the usual classes. Instead, I would arrange a daily piano lesson and the rest of the day he was to practice. Mine was a boarding school, and I told him that when he wrote home, he was not to tell his parents what he was doing.

At the end of the term there was a speech day; all the boys sat in front and all of the parents were at the back of the hall. Halfway through the proceedings, I announced that there would be a very special musical interlude. The eleven-year-old for whom I had arranged music lessons climbed up onto the platform and rendered, on the piano, a selection of classical music that was so well played it stunned all those present, including two amazed parents. The applause was deafening.

The boy bowed with a huge smile, having completed his mission of learning to play the piano. How he enjoyed the feeling of satisfaction for becoming a master at what he loved to do. He demonstrated the principle of completion, which is always followed by gratification and a strong sense of contentment. It is the seventh personal power. Now, my eleven-year-old student, having successfully proved his ability on the piano, was able to return to his normal studies at which he became successful, inspired by his musical achievement.

Once you have mastered one situation, it becomes easier to do well and to develop your ability in another area. That is why it is beneficial to praise a child for a small accomplishment, which in turn will lead to larger results down the line. No different than a young child, you as an adult need to start with assignments you enjoy performing, so that your personal power of completion will quickly find a satisfactory conclusion. The gratification and enjoyment you gain will provide the impetus for you to go from strength to strength, from completion to completion and from satisfaction to satisfaction for the rest of your life.

Completion, your seventh personal power is the culmination of the understanding and use of your first six personal powers. It focuses on the ending of a task, when the mission is fulfilled. This is the time to reflect, to look back on the steps you had to climb to accomplish an end result. Completion only takes place when the first six steps I've presented are properly executed. In fact, results from action you have taken in your personal life are in direct proportion to your understanding and application of your personal powers one through six.

Let's quickly review the seven steps or personal powers we've examined here. They are also called the Seven Natural Laws.

There are different types of laws that maintain order on the planet Earth. Man-made laws such as traffic regulations keep our society orderly. If a policeman observes you speeding on a highway, he will probably give you a speeding ticket. Scientific principles such as gravity keep our planet orderly. If you release an object midair, it will fall to the ground. There is another set of laws, natural laws, which, when observed, provide health, wealth, happiness, loving relationships and right occupations. If these conditions are not the normal state of life for you, then a natural law is probably not being observed.

"But," you may protest, "I understand most traffic and scientific laws. I'm not sure about these natural laws, so I can't possibly be responsible for them." Nonsense! Ignorance of a law does not mean that it does not exist. Do you think that if you tell a police officer you do not know the speed limit he will not give you a ticket? Or that because you had not yet discovered the law of gravity the object would not drop to the floor? Of course not!

Number One — The Law of Oneness

Law number one is based on the number one: We are all one. Remember? I discussed oneness in the first chapter. The four kingdoms of life — human, animal, vegetable and mineral — all are created by the same God-source and are of that God-energy. Humanity is the only element that does not understand this oneness. As such, it is the only element that is out of sync. The symbol of oneness is the circle. When two people get married, what is the outward symbol? A ring. It symbolizes that they have become one. There is no beginning and there is no end.

In the Catholic Church, a woman is initiated by a ring ceremony when she becomes a nun: She inwardly marries Christ, and a ring is put on her finger to symbolize that as a nun she has become one with God.

And our planet Earth is a circular planet. When astronauts describe it from outer space, they talk about the simplicity, the roundness, the smallness of the planet. And they say they cannot conceive how countries could ever quarrel on such a peaceful-looking globe.

But there are many people who are not aware of the concept of oneness. Oneness cannot be legislated; it can only be demonstrated. Those who have a sense of oneness will have to demonstrate it, live it, and be such an example that others will ascribe to it, too.

Number Two — The Law of Duality and Balance

The second law comes straight out of one and becomes two, because that one energy is dual by nature. It is scientifically referred to as centripetal/centrifugal power. Electricity, for example, uses two wires: one red and positive, and one black, negative. In only one wire, there is no flow of electricity. It takes two wires to generate power. Likewise in life you need to combine male and female to

stimulate a balanced flow of energy. In the East, it is called
the yin and yang, and this is the symbol of law number two.
When I presented the fascinating story of Peter and Eileen
Caddy, you were able to read first hand about two remarkable people who symbolized the yin and the yang, the law
of number two.

There are two aspects of our being: the outgoing part,
which is the masculine, the doing; and the incoming part,
which is the feminine, the intuition. The female is the wise
one, because it is the part that knows; women are intuitive
and inspirational. The masculine represents love: males are
the lovers and love is the highest energy that can be given.
Once we know that both the masculine and the feminine
natures exist in us whether we are men or women, we can
work to develop both of our own natures to create a balance.

This concept can be put another way: the love and the
life. Life is the female beingness, the mother, and love is the
male, the outgoing doingness, the father. And the balance
we are aiming for is moving love through our lives. It is
symbolized in all the great religions: in Judaic teachings, by
the two pillars outside Solomon's temple; in the Catholic
Church, by the two large candles on the altar symbolizing
the male love and the female wisdom balanced.

Number Three — The Law of Creativity

The third law comes from the second law: When you
take love and move it through life, you get the result —
light. For instance, when a man and woman have inter-
course, they create a child. Another way to look at it is that
the interaction of male love with female intuition results in
ideas. When you are doing what you love — when you love
your work — the light of happiness will be the manifestation. We are on Earth to give out intuitive talent to the
world: the painter who paints creates pictures; the baker

who bakes creates bread; the writer who writes creates books. The question is: What are we going to create? What light are we going to give to the world?

"But," you may say, "I don't have a natural talent. I'm not a genius." The dictionary defines the word "genius" as natural ability. Everyone has a natural ability; a recognized genius merely knows what his natural ability is and uses it. You have only to claim your genius power to fulfill your highest good. I discuss finding the "genius within" in Chapter Three.

The symbol for law number three is the equilateral triangle, representing that the father–mother–child or love–life–light components are equally important. The third cannot exist without the other two.

Number Four — The Law of the Fourfold Nature of Man

There are four parts to man's consciousness. The first three are the physical, which is the lowest; the emotional, which is a little higher and controls the physical; and the mental, which controls the emotional. The fourth and highest state of consciousness is the spiritual, which controls the mind. As I have explained earlier, the good news is that we can control our thoughts by entering the fourth, spiritual state. As I have observed in this chapter, this is the most powerful state; it controls the mind, which controls the emotions, which control the body. It is our God-power which is not dual by nature but just is. When we are in touch with spiritual perfection, we will think right, feel right and act right. This is what *Inward Bound* is all about: attaining this fourth state of consciousness and bringing our four bodies — spiritual, mental, emotional and physical — into balance.

I want you to understand that you have this power. And when you realize it, your whole life changes from that moment. It did for me. I've never been the same since. Because I realize I can do anything I want, any time I want, because I accept that this spiritual, perfect God-power is within. And you can do likewise.

The symbol of the balanced, fourfold nature of man is the weather vane, symbolizing the cardinal points of the compass: the physical in the west, the spiritual in the east, the mental in the north and the emotional in the south.

Number Five — The Law of the Five Senses of Man

The five senses — sight, hearing, smell, taste and touch — are gateways that operate through the four natures of man — physical, emotional, mental and spiritual. Each of us actually has twenty senses: each of the five gateways operating through each of the four natures. For example, take the sense of hearing and apply it to one of my classes. Everyone hears me physically because I have a powerful voice. It is very hard to sleep during my lectures. Some hear me emotionally because I get excited and wave my arms about, which excites them, too. Some hear me mentally and take notes for future reference. And some will hear me spiritually, for when I say something, they might say, "Oh, yes! That's right!" They wake up to what they already know though they have never heard it before. That is because they already know it deep within and that is knowing it spiritually.

There's a story in the Old Testament about Samuel when he was a little boy. His mother Hannah took him up to the temple when he was seven years of age to present him to God to be a priest. Samuel's teacher was Eli.

One night when the little boy was asleep, he heard a voice calling him, "Samuel! Samuel! Sam-u-el!" So, very obediently, he got out of bed and ran to his teacher. "Did you call me?" he asked. "I didn't. Go back to bed, young man." The little boy went back to bed.

It happened a second time and then a third. Samuel got out of bed each time and ran to Eli. The third time, Eli said, "Wait a minute! I understand what's happening! The next time you hear the voice, answer: 'Speak, Lord, for thy servant heareth.'" Well, the little boy went back to bed.

Sure enough, the voice came: "Samuel! Samuel! Samu-el!" So he said, "Speak, Lord, for thy servant heareth." And at that moment, God gave him two messages: one, what was going to happen to his teacher, Eli; and two, what was going to happen to him, Samuel, when he grew up.

You see, he had to hear it four times before he got the point. Which translated to reality means: maybe you have to read this book four times before you get it!

The symbol of the five gateways is the five-pointed star.

Number Six — The Law of Work

One of the major principles of the laws of life is that you have to W-O-R-K! If you are disappointed to hear this, you probably do not know what the word "work" really means. Unfortunately, we are brought up to believe that work is something you do Monday through Friday so that you can have pleasure Saturday and Sunday.

Actually, work and pleasure should be identical. When you love your daily occupation, your work becomes your pleasure. The people who are really creative and productive do not stop work at five o'clock. They never wait to start again on Monday morning. They are doing it all the time because they love it. People who enjoy their work are happy, productive, and they make money. Until we find the work in life that we want to do, the genius that is our gift, we will not be happy.

The number six symbolizes work. For instance, what was the first thing Jesus did at the beginning of his ministry? He changed six jars of water into wine at the wedding at Cana, the number six symbolizing that he was ready for his work. Solomon had to climb six steps before he sat on the throne to become the wise man he was. And how many days did it take God to create the world? Six. The seventh day, he rested. All religions respect this law and provide a day of rest — whether it is the Christian Sunday, the Jewish Saturday or the Muslim Friday.

So how many days should we work? Six! We should be giving of ourselves constantly — not just the four or five days a week (or as little as we can). The seventh day is to recharge our batteries, to just relax.

The symbol for law number six is the Star of David, which existed in Egypt long before Abraham was born or the Jewish nation was founded. It actually consists of two triangles. The first triangle, representing creativity at the inner level, is inverted over the other, representing creativity manifested at the outer level.

Number Seven — The Law of Completion

The seventh and last law really is not a law at all. It is a summary of the six: The capstone of completion turning back to one. That is why seven is considered the sacred spiritual number.

We start with one, the God-energy; realize it is dual in nature *(two)*, which is the masculine and feminine. We realize when we combine these, we go to *three* and become creative. We realize we have *four* bodies to express that creativity. We have *five* channels through which to learn and know. *Six,* we manifest through work. *Seven,* we are complete and whole.

As you can see, your seven personal powers are the same as the Seven Laws of the Universe.

Briefly, then, to recapitulate, you come from the understanding of oneness, which consists of the duality of

incoming and outgoing energy. You combine these two
personal powers so that you become creative. Realizing that
you have four bodies available for use and five gateways
through which you can be aware of everything, you go to
work doing what you love the most, to manifest great
results in your life. Finally, you reap satisfaction through
your personal power of completion. The word completion
literally means bringing together all the parts to fulfill the
result required. Your first six personal powers are like six
parts that blend together for you to live a life of perfection.
If you fail to use one of the six powers, your life will be
lacking something.

For example, you may understand the need to balance
male love with female intuition. You even use your five
senses and are prepared to work hard. You do apply the
power of oneness and the win–win concept. Then you
wonder why your life does not work. It doesn't work
because you left out your understanding of creativity and
the fourfold nature of man. You will only be successful,
fulfilled and happy when you use all your personal powers.
Suppose you are baking a cake and the recipe calls for seven
ingredients and you leave one out, namely the flour. It is
very obvious that your cake will be a dismal failure. The
same applies in your life. There is a fundamental recipe for
life that calls for the use of your first seven powers in
combination, but if you leave one out, then your expectation
of success will suffer.

Let's look at nature for an example that illustrates
failure when a key ingredient is missing from the growing
cycle. Plant a seed in fertile soil, water it, expose it to fresh
air and sunlight, and the result will be a seedling that
develops into a healthy and productive plant. However, if
you don't water the seed and it dries up, nothing happens. A

seed has everything built into it for growth and survival. All it needs are the right conditions of sunlight, fresh air, water and fertile soil in order to flourish. In the same way, you and I have everything within us in the form of personal powers to be successful. But these powers must be engaged, as the following story demonstrates.

The parents of young boy met with an accident and were killed in the Australian outback, leaving their ten-year-old son alone to fend for himself in the bush.

Completely lost and frantic about how he was going to find food and survive all on his own, the boy discovered on his second day an old man living in the desolate country. He asked the old man for food, but the crusty old recluse refused. Tearfully, the boy said, "Don't you understand I am hungry and I need food?" But the old man ignored the youngster.

In desperation, the boy followed the old man. The next day, he watched how he gathered berries and caught a fish with his hands in a shallow pool of water. Thus, the ten-year-old learned how to find his own food to survive.

Then one day the young boy caught, all on his own, a big fish. He built a fire, cooked the fish, and was just about to eat it, when the old man came over to see what he was doing. The boy pointed his finger at the old man and said, "You go and catch your own fish!"

You and I are sometimes like this young boy. We would prefer somebody else to do it for us, whether it is gathering food or being creative and actively involved in work that makes us fulfilled and successful. However, if you wake up to the fact that it is all a matter of taking responsibility for yourself, actively being engaged in an occupation you love, you may succeed far beyond your dreams.

In ages gone by, there were "Mystery Schools." which taught the secrets of life to chosen pupils who were admitted to learn of the esoteric. We now live in a day and age when all will be made known, and you have come to realize that you are potentially a powerful person and are prepared to use the seven personal powers so far described in this book to manifest the power of one as part of the greater oneness of the universe.

The symbol for completion, your seventh personal power, is the rainbow. The rainbow is made up of seven different colors, one color for each of your personal powers. It is created by passing white light through a prism. This crystalline body breaks down the white light into seven different rays, just as when the sun shines through the rain under certain conditions to create a rainbow in the sky. The rainbow is sevenfold in nature, yet it comes from one. In the same way, you have seven personal powers, which come together in the seventh power of completion. It is interesting to note that many businesses today are using the concept of the rainbow in their logos, in their advertising, and on business cards.

The number seven is a perfectly whole, spiritual number. God created the world in seven days, there are seven days in a week and human beings are sevenfold in their nature. Eastern philosophy and religion describe the seven chakra vortice points of power in your physical body, which represent your seven levels of consciousness. The lowest chakra is at the base of the spine. Moving up the spine, power points are found in the area of the sexual organs, the solar plexus, the heart, the throat area, the third eye, and the seventh and last chakra is at the top of the head. Seven is considered to be a spiritual number and, by some people, seven is thought of as a lucky number.

When I was young and used to drive on the track, I remember from those days that Stirling Moss was a famous motor racing driver in England. He always insisted that his racing car be marked with the number seven. Throughout history, in many places, by many people, seven has held great meaning.

There are seven precious jewels, which represent the seven colors of the rainbow in a solid form; the red ruby, the orange sardius, the yellow topaz, the green emerald, the blue sapphire, the purple amethyst-sapphire and the pure violet amethyst. These seven precious jewels together with five semiprecious jewels were worn on a breastplate by Melchizedek, the high priest of Israel, representing the twelve tribes of Israel. The names of the jewels are listed in the Holy Bible.

In music there are seven notes on the piano: A, B, C, D, E, F, G. The seven notes correspond to the vibration of the colors of the rainbow. C is red, D is orange, E is yellow, F is green, G is blue, A is purple, B is violet. Music played in the key of C is very physical, military-type music; on the other hand, music played in the key of B is spiritual, violet, saintly type of music. There are also five semitones, the five black keys which, when added to seven, make twelve. There is much hidden knowledge that links together color, music, precious jewels, the chakra points and other phenomena. On examination, one discovers that the number seven is found in many places because it represents the total, the completion in any one area of life.

The word "complete" is synonymous with the word "whole," which is another word for health. When you are healthy, you are whole and complete. The word "heal" means to make healthy or whole. When you are in the state of health, you are in a state of oneness. In fact, this seventh power of completion is all about being in perfect health. The normal condition of a person is to be healthy. However, so many people become sick and ill that there are those who believe that a state of unwellness is more natural than the state of health. Such an idea reflects the negativism of people who cannot accept the idea of responsibility for self rising out of spiritual wholeness.

As I have become more aware of how the physical body works, I do not get sick. I do not have headaches, catch a cold or get the flu. Why not? Simply because I practice preventive medicine. I live in such a way that I remain healthy. If your immune system is functioning properly, it will prevent your body from becoming ill. The air you breathe on a daily basis is full of germs, but if your immune system is functioning properly, it will destroy these germs. However, if the immune system is in a weakened condition, watch out. Aside from external influences, negative thinking, fear and stress all weaken the immune system. So in order to keep the immune system strong and healthy, you should be positive in your thinking, relaxed, calm and at ease.

Some twenty years ago, I met Carl Simonton, a medical doctor who works with cancer patients. We became good friends and it was Carl who explained to me how cancer works. Carl Simonton wrote the book *Getting Well Again.* Everybody, including you and me, gets cancer on a regular basis. This is called clinical cancer. However, provided your immune system is functioning properly, your white blood cells swallow up the cancer cells and they will be destroyed, instead of multiplying rapidly as they too often do to form a dangerous growth. Therefore, one of the best ways to ensure good health is to keep your immune system working properly. This is done largely by right thinking, proper exercise and a good diet.

How do you make sure that you perform properly in these areas? Remember, you have four bodies or levels of consciousness: spiritual, mental, emotional, and physical. Activate the spiritual and the other three bodies will follow suit. So, listen to your intuition, the voice within, at your spiritual level. To the degree that you tune into your intuition, so will you receive proper guidance. In my own life, as a result of inner guidance, I was led to become a vegetarian at a very early age in life. I was only twelve years old when I quit eating meat. Since then I have refined my dietary habits, eating less fat and as much as possible avoiding mucous-forming foods such as cheese. No more candy bars, coffee and soft drinks. I do not smoke and only indulge in a glass of wine on special occasions. I enjoy lots of fruit, fiber, fresh salads, steamed vegetables, pasta, grains and breads. I only drink water and fruit juices. I exercise regularly and my intuition ever leads and guides me to eat in the most natural way possible. I am well over seventy years of age and am in excellent health.

Last, but not least, in order to keep my immune system functioning in a proper manner, I pay attention to how I think. I do this by sitting still at the start of every day, so that I may quiet my outer, intellectual thinking and go deeper into my fourth body level, my spiritual level where I activate my intuition. This peaceful state prevents worry and stress. This technique is called centering and is described in detail in Chapter Ten. Everybody needs to take time out on a daily basis to practice a method of relaxation, meditation or any procedure that takes you into a tranquil state of consciousness. This above all else will help to keep your immune system working in a proper manner.

The secret of life is to go as deeply as possible within in one direction so that you are able to produce the maximum results in the other, outer direction of the physical world. There is a saying, "As within, so without."

This will bring about satisfaction and completion in your life. Many people are out of balance because they are always concerned with the outer results in the materialistic, physical world of making as much money as possible. These people give little attention to what causes the results. To be truly successful, you need to spend much time in dreaming, creating a vision, making plans, setting definite goals, imaging and visualizing. That is if you desire to enjoy the fruits of completion.

Nature is a wonderful example of the seventh power of completion. Everything in nature is in balance and therefore is complete. Consider the earth, how the trees grow and shed their leaves on the ground, which decay, turn into humus and replenish the soil, so that seeds can sprout and grow in the earth to once more become trees. The cycle of nature is in balance, it is complete. Even the animal life becomes involved, from the tiny insects that help to break down the fallen branches, to bees that pollinate the flowers and the birds that spread the seeds from place to place.

As important as it is to get our outer and inner worlds into balance, so is it equally important that we work with the four natural kingdoms, namely mineral, vegetable, animal and human. It is good to know that we are waking up to the need to study ecology and to work with the environment, so that we and the world will be balanced, become one, and enter the seventh state of satisfaction and completion.

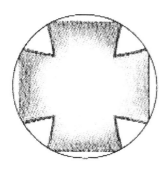

Chapter Eight

Service

The bird sings the secret of life, "Life is service." To live is to sing your own song by using your gift in service to others.

Guru Nanak

In his splendid book, *Awakening the Buddha Within,* Lama Surya Das, an American born student of the natural and spiritual, whose Anglo-Saxon name was Jeffrey Miller, made a definition all of us should take to heart:

"How many hours of your day do you spend on a treadmill of activity trying to get what you think you want? At what point do all those endless hours spell out obsession? How much of your mind and time is spent fantasizing about the things you desire? It's all too easy to use up most of the hours in our lives being obsessed with romance, career, money, unrequited or turbulent love, hobbies, sex, or

pleasure. Like a muddy cloud, craving obscures your unfet-
tered, radiant spiritual nature.

"In this culture, who can resist an almost mindless
thirst for sensual pleasures, wealth, or power? There are so
many billboards, so many advertisements, and so many
shopping malls grabbing our attention. Don't you often feel
buffeted by the gusts of 'coming attractions' clamoring for
your attention?"

In a following statement, Lama Surya Das describes
the method by which we can rid ourselves of the craving:

"There is a one-word antidote to thirst or craving:
wisdom. The wisdom of freedom from craving. The secret
teachings of Tibet tell us that we can rediscover our innate
wisdom, awareness, and inner joy through spiritual
practices, including meditation, self-inquiry, prayer, and the
cultivation of our naturally warm, tender loving heart.
Wisdom is the means to transcend craving and transform a
treadmill existence into a lovely, inspiring garden walk.
This is true freedom."

Implicit in the idea of freedom, as defined by Lama
Surya Das, is the word "service," the eighth personal power.
This power can come to all of us when the work we perform
is done with an attitude of giving. Service come from the
Latin word *servus,* which means a slave. Webster's dictionary defines service as the occupation of a servant. In
England, when I was young, to be "in service" implied that
you were a domestic servant such as a butler, valet,
chauffeur, housekeeper, parlor or kitchen maid. The British
television series *Upstairs, Downstairs* superbly illustrates
the meaning of being "in service." The implication is
obvious; when you are in service to another person, you are
helping and placing that person before and above yourself.
You are literally the servant of the one you are helping and

serving. But the important point to remember is that when you perform your work with a strong attitude of goodwill for other people, for those you are serving, then your action will return to you in the form of blessings and rewards you never could have anticipated.

Today, people too often seem less concerned with service. Most people are more concerned with how much money they will make, what position in the company they will hold. Perhaps that is why so many people are not very successful. They don't understand the secret of serving — how it returns to the giver far more than he expends of himself. In order to become fulfilled, prosperous and successful, you have to perform your work in a spirit of service. You need to put the other person first.

Service is part of the idea of self-transformation that we looked at earlier in the book. And, as Lama Surya Das reminds us, "Self-transformation implies self-transcendence. Therefore, inner transformation is a spiritual affair of cosmic significance, including all animate and inanimate, everywhere. Authentic self-transformation is definitely not for oneself alone. It is for all beings — for aren't we all inseparably interconnected? Whatever befalls us, befalls one and all; harm a single strand of the web of life, and the entire web is harmed. In Africa, the Xhosa tribe has a saying which is worth remembering: 'I am because we are.'"

If you think of service in this grand sense, "I am because we are," then you will have come a long way down the path of your own self-transcendence.

The stories about the late Mother Teresa have always been an inspiration and an example of service for me to follow. Mother Teresa devoted her life in India to the service of others, in particular, the destitute, the sick and the dying. She understood that service was part of the path to self-transcendence. She owned nothing herself, yet had all that she needed. Wherever she went, people gave her money, homes to live in, cars for transportation and food and supplies for her work with the poor. Mother Teresa personally was never in need of anything.

At one point in her life, she contemplated retiring, but her immediate followers voted that she should continue to run her order. To her dying day, Mother Teresa continued to be in service to those less fortunate than herself. Now it is unlikely that we are all going to become a Mother Teresa. However, you can look at the principles she practiced and adopt her way of service to some degree in the work you perform.

Many people have enjoyed reading the Arthurian legends. The stories about King Arthur and his knights are all about service and they give us an inner meaning which many can apply in a practical way to their own lives. First of all, King Arthur and his knights sat around a circular table that represented equality and oneness. The work of the knights was always directed to helping people in difficulties, such as rescuing a fair damsel in distress. The knights were always in service to others. They carried a sword with which to destroy the enemy. The sword represented the flame of love, which had the power to cut down and thereby purify and cleanse wrong conditions.

Likewise, when you work and serve with love, you will be able to help others and put conditions right that may be out of balance. In the early Middle Ages, there were many knighthood orders that protected the Crusaders on the way to the Holy Land. Their work was to serve the travelers who wished to go to the Holy Land for an inner, spiritual experience. The knights built hospices and refuges to aid the sick and injured and so became, indirectly, the founders of our modern day hospitals.

As a young man interested in architecture and photography before World War II, I used to take detailed photographs of old churches, among which was the Temple Church near the Law Courts in London. It had been built by the Knights Templar. This church was destroyed by bombs and fire during the blitz of World War II. I was honored to serve the reconstruction of the church by submitting my photographs to the builders. At this time, there is a revival of this knighthood order and their teachings of service. There are also the Knights of Malta, whose emblem is the Maltese Cross, which these knights emblazoned on their shields.

The Maltese Cross is the symbol of your personal power of service. The best way to describe this symbol is to say that is is made up of four fish's tails joined together at the center and projecting outward as four arms in the shape of a cross, where all four arms are of equal length. Each of the fish's tails has two points; and since four multiplied by two makes eight, these eight points represent the power of service. The generally accepted reason for the fish's tails as an emblem was that it was designed and first used in the time of the "Astrological Age of Pisces the Fish."

The knights who were active at the time of the Crusades in the Holy Land built a unique church in Segovia, Spain, close to the monastery of Saint John of the Cross. This church was built in the shape of an octagon, an eight-sided building, another reminder that eight represents the service that these knights used to perform. There is much wisdom and knowledge to be found concerning service when you delve into past history. Today, we need to revive the power of service.

The word "service" has become a buzz word in the marketplace. Perhaps, at last, we are coming to realize the need to serve.

In many instances, the service being performed is obvious. For example, a secretary serves the boss, a nurse serves the patient, a waiter serves the customer, a teacher serves the pupil, a writer serves the reader, a lawyer serves the client, an airplane pilot serves the passengers, a medical doctor serves the patients, a policeman serves the public, an auto mechanic serves the car owner, and the list goes on and on. The trick to having a successful life is take your job, however mundane, and orient it in the direction of service.

I came to realize happily that the influence I have had on many people will survive me as a spiritual teacher. Likewise, you too can send out in your life an energy that becomes so deeply ingrained in what you are doing that it will continue indefinitely, like waves that travel across the world. Good acts of service to others have repercussions that influence others long after they are first initiated.

Earlier in this chapter I described the services to humanity to which Mother Teresa devoted her life. I met this remarkable woman in India and saw in her being the love of God demonstrated in her every thought. Though she was nearing ninety years old, Mother Teresa never seemed overwhelmed or exhausted by her tasks of helping others. And, of course, the reason is that she was inspired by God. Her strength came from the energy of her faith, her passion.

But others of us, who have not learned the real secret of the process of self renewal find ourselves burned out. Burnout and recovery were described by Brian Luke Seaward in his book *Stand Like Mountain, Flow Like Water:*

"Sad to say that the most common coping techniques for burnout are nothing that remotely resemble self-renewal. Instead, people opt for quick fixes and stimulation through alcohol, drugs and other addictive substances.

Initially, these may look appealing; however, spiritual energy cannot be replaced through material means or physical substances. These only drain the human spirit through illusion and deception.

"Self-renewal is a continual process, and we must constantly strive to replenish the energy of spirit. It is as important as breathing. To be present and attentive to those around us, to be strong for others in times of need, we must look after our own well-being first. Without strength and endurance, we run the risk of pulling everyone down with us when the pressures of life become overwhelming."

Having described the deficit we humans often impose upon ourselves by failing to renew our resources, Seaward goes on to describe the fundamental lack from which so many of us suffer — the same lack that Mother Teresa never knew:

"We must attend to our own source of personal energy so that we may be available to others in times of need. At first this notion may seem to contradict the Christian ethic of placing others before yourself, but a closer look reveals there is no contradiction whatsoever. The golden rule reminds us to love others as ourselves. This equation of human conduct has become lopsided because most people, in placing others first [the idea of service] grow accustomed to ignoring their own needs. Cultural influences imply that taking time to love and honor ourselves is selfish, even sinful. But by neglecting our own needs, we pave the way for feelings of frustration and victimization.

"The art of self-renewal is neither selfish nor ego-enhancing. Instead, it gives us permission to appreciate and love ourselves. When we feel good about ourselves we have something of quality to give, instead of offering empty gestures, insincere actions or conditional love."

Seaward reminds us that it was author Leo Buscaglia who wrote:

"When you love yourself, you will love others. And to the depth and extent to which you can love yourself, only to that depth and extent will you be able to love others."

Seaward furnishes us with a vision of the self-transcended human who can *Stand Like Mountain, Flow Like Water.*

"To stand like mountain is the ability to recognize the potential of our inner resources. To flow like water is to act on this potential. Our inner resources are not gifts for a chosen few as much as they are birthrights for everyone. Every day we are called upon to use and expand our potential by employing these inner resources. Our spiritual potential, as expressed through humor, compassion, faith, forgiveness, courage, creativity and intuition, is like a group of instruments. Our spiritual health is demonstrated when we play those instruments. With practice, we are all capable of making beautiful music. Life may be a journey, but with God as the maestro, it is also a marvelous symphony."

The opposite of service, as embodied in a selfish or hurtful act directed at another person, is like the ripples in a pond traveling from the splash point inward instead of outward. All good actions, as I noted, continue indefinitely in an outward direction. However, if you perform a negative, bad action and do someone a dis-service, the opposite takes place. Instead of the ripples going in an outward direction, they turn inward pressing upon you like a stigmata upon your soul, bringing a feeling of depression. Loving thoughts go outward to help others. Hateful thoughts and worry turn in upon yourself and you suffer from them.

As a guide to providing service, read the seven points written below. These seven steps I created to help teach salespeople how to become more successful. However, they apply equally well in all walks of life.

1. "Be relaxed." People are aware of the way you are when they come into your orbit of influence. You need to set the stage and create an attitude of openness and acceptance. People feel the energy you give out such as the charisma that flows from your presence. Remember, "What you are speaks so loudly that people don't always hear what you say." Being calm and relaxed is the way to go.

2. "Timing is vital." People don't listen if something else is on their minds. Generally speaking, the early part of the day works best, when you have a clear mind, and energy and enthusiasm flows more freely. I have observed that students at my seminars listen and learn more in the morning sessions than after lunch or in the evening. The salesperson needs to make breakfast appointments in preference to lunch or dinner meetings. You are more eager and alert to obtain results in the earlier part of the day.

3. "Quality counts." You, yourself, need to be well groomed and neatly dressed. Your appearance is extremely important. The atmosphere and elegance of the place of meeting, such as a good restaurant, creates an ambiance and sense of well-being that effects the outcome of the service you are offering. Check out your office and if you are interviewing a person, get out from behind your desk. Don't allow the desk to become a barrier between you and your customer or client.

4. "Talk quietly." Speak slowly and pronounce your words so that every syllable is heard. Once in a while, for emphasis, you can raise your voice and

speak more rapidly. However, overall, to make sure that the listener understands what you say, speak clearly and slowly. The art of good communication is to be as direct as possible and use short and simple words. You can't be in service to another person if what you say is not understood!

5.   "Ask questions," such as, "Do you need more information?" "Do you understand what I have said?" or "How can I serve you better?" The more questions that you ask, the better you will be able to be of service to the other person. Keep the questions going. Remember that in sales, the customer will only buy when you have answered all his questions.

6.   "Listen, listen and listen." A good listener offers the greatest service. It is only by listening that you can truly help another person. Years ago, a woman came to visit me to ask my advice on a certain matter. She talked and talked and I listened and listened. I never said a word and after an hour was up she said, "I must go now." She thanked me profusely for helping her and I had never said a word! To serve another person is not too difficult. Often all you have to do is listen. This especially holds good in the field of sales. The customer that talks the most is most likely to buy. The salesperson who listens the most is most likely to sell.

7.   "Create a bond." The greater and stronger the connection you make with the other person, the more that person will receive from you. A sense of security will pervade. If you are in sales, you can offer a guarantee and point out the merits of the after-sale service your firm offers. Create a bond of friendship between yourself and your customer.

Serve with a smile on your face and let customers know that you truly care about them. Outline how you will keep in touch with them. Impress on the customer your sincere desire to serve. Place a seal upon your sale. Create a bond between the two of you. Then repeat business and further sales are sure to follow.

Whatever work you perform, the common word that links your service to others is the word "love." Love is the energy that should permeate everything you do. Love is the outgoing, masculine energy, the centrifugal force that spreads out like the ripples on a pond. Likewise, when you sling a pebble, your contribution, into the pond of life with love, you make invisible ripples that flow to the ends of the earth.

To provide service to others does not require a great effort or a long exploration. Spiritually, service to others is based on your own passage to the light, on your path to self-transcendence, which Lama Surya Das addressed in memorable words:

"One need not travel to distant lands, seek exotic mystical experiences, master esoteric mantras and treatises, or cultivate extraordinary states of mind in order to experience a radical change of heart and inner transformation. Spiritually speaking, everything that one wants, aspires to, and needs is ever-present, accessible here and now — for those with eyes to see. It's the old adage all over again: You don't need to see different things, but rather to see things differently."

"World Service" is a plan I recently conceived and it is already being used by a number of my students. However, if this concept is carried out on a large enough scale, it could establish a lasting peace on planet Earth. This is not as difficult as it might sound. It merely requires enough like-minded people to be dedicated to the development and practice of service. Details regarding the basis of World Service are printed in Appendix A.

The application of World Service by enough individuals could bring peace to the world. The reasoning is quite simple: If everybody were busy serving and helping others, it would be impossible for them to fight and make war. If you are doing something constructive, you can't be doing something destructive at the same time. For example, when I first started teaching in England, I learned very quickly how to create silence in the classroom. I told my students to take out their history book and start reading at page ten. If they were busy reading, they couldn't be talking and making noise. Some less enlightened teachers, on entering the classroom, would tell the students to shut up. Since no student knew what shut up meant, they went on making a noise.

Adults do not understand how not to have a war. However, if everybody in the world is busy serving his fellow man, no war could happen or exist. To serve others is constructive; it is that simple. Serving is the best way you can share with another soul. You may be saying, "I am not a teacher, my work does not seem so important." Not so. Whatever your job is in life, however simple and humble it may appear to be, it is your contribution, your way of serving. Nobody but you, yourself, can do what you do best. In fact, you are cheating the world if you fail to share with others your unique gift and talent that is yours alone.

To find the service that will suit you, get in touch with who you are. Present your work as service to others. It is useful to return to the words of Lama Surya Das for a final definition of service:

"Right effort is not always goal- and achievement-oriented; it also includes the subtler virtues of nondoing, of yielding, and going with the greater flow. When Paul McCartney sang *Let It Be,* we all responded to his words. Through right effort we learn how to do the best we can in life, living fully and with all our heart — and then let go, knowing that whatever happens, happens. The universe is beyond our control, anyway. Trying to control things creates more stress, struggle, and irritating friction in the greater system.

"This balanced combination of effort, inner detachment, and genuine equanimity helps us to come home within ourselves, and arrive at a feeling of inner peace and oneness...."

When you have achieved oneness, the quality of your service to others will assume great stature, much like a memory of goodness that is passed on from generation to generation.

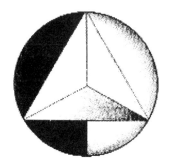

Chapter
Nine

Prosperity

Those who resent the rich are usually poor.
Dennis Stephenson

Your ninth personal power is the power of prosperity: how to manifest wealth, to make sufficient money and create enough cash. My question to you is, "Are you making a living or are you making a dying?" In other words, are you producing enough money so that you are able to live comfortably, meet all your needs and have sufficient cash set aside for your retirement and old age, or are you finding it hard to pay your bills, struggling to survive and unable to save funds to live to a great age? According to statistics from the Social Security Administration, as many as seventy-five percent of the people in the United States depend on relatives and charity when they reach the age of sixty-five. Twenty percent keep working because they can't afford to retire and only five percent or less are self sustaining. It seems that the majority of us are trying to survive, and only a small minority are financially independent and are making a living.

The previous chapter was all about service, so it is a natural sequence that this chapter should be concerned with manifesting the results you create as a result of the service you perform from the work you do. I will use my own life as an example of how you can become financially sound and secure. Then, I will list some practical guidelines for you to follow, so that you may have the money you need to be independent and self sustaining in your old age.

After the end of World War II, I became a school teacher and eventually founded Shiplake College at Henly on Thames in England. At a later date, I arranged to have this educational establishment turned into a "charitable trust" to preserve its identity and ensure its future indefinitely. Shortly afterward, I traveled around the world seeking a greater challenge in my life. I decided to settle in the United States, and I arrived on a liner, the Queen Mary, in New York with no capital and only a hundred or so dollars in my pocket. I was bound for Unity Village near Kansas City, where I would work and develop spiritual growth. There I was contacted by the headmaster of the Country Day School in Kansas City and invited by him to help set up a new private day school in Fort Worth, Texas. My profession as a teacher in the private school system made this job offer easy for me to accept, and at forty years old, I arrived in Texas with virtually nothing to support myself. During the next sixteen years, I used my personal power to prosper by orchestrating a series of events to create what I needed in my life.

My first requirement was to have a roof over my head. Because I had no money for a down payment to purchase a house, I had no alternative but to rent an apartment. I did not want to use my monthly salary for rent, because it would prevent me from saving to buy my own house, so I found an empty garage apartment behind a duplex. The property was in disarray with a filthy, dirty carpet and a front door that was off its hinges. The building was a disgrace — broken and dirty windows, paint peeling off the walls and garbage in the back yard. I found the owner and struck a deal that I could have the garage apartment rent-free if I repaired it, managed two other duplexes, collected the rent and maintained the property.

By not having to pay rent, I saved enough money from my salary that within five years I had the necessary cash for a down payment on my own home. Then I quit teaching school, worked in the restaurant business and started my own program, Mind Dynamics, seminars for adults on developing brain power. Within three years, I left Texas and moved to San Francisco, where I bought an old fixer-up type of house in the Avenues, adjacent to Golden Gate Park. This was a terrace-type house, only twenty-five feet wide with living quarters above a double wide-garage. There was a handkerchief-sized garden at the rear of the property. I made a deposit of $4,000 on this $24,000 property. I set up my Mind Dynamics seminars in the back room of a friend's office in San Rafael. I worked five days a week in the office and taught seminars on the weekends. I built a reputation as a teacher of adults, created a successful business, moved into my own premises and went from strength to strength. After eight years of living in San Francisco, building a world-wide program of education and a reputation as "the man responsible for inspiring the human potential movement in the United States," I decided to move on. I quit Mind Dynamics and created a more spiritual type of program called Inward Bound, the same title as that of this book. I still teach it to this day in a modified form. During my eight years in San Francisco, I worked on my little house with love and care. I was able to sell this wreck of a house converted to a modern, charming residence for almost $100,000, which was four times what I had paid for it in the first place.

With this money, I bought property near Eugene, Oregon. In reality, I exchanged a twenty-five-foot-wide house for twenty-five acres of land, plus an older home, a couple of barns, a small lake and many trees in the green and pleasant land of Oregon. This older, country home has been added to, fully repaired, repainted, reroofed and remodeled. This small estate now includes new out buildings, a large, fenced vegetable garden complete with grape arbor, a small orchard and much fencing. The value of this property has increased by leaps and bounds. All this came about over a thirty-year period by my starting with a few dollars in my pocket when I arrived in the United States from the old country of England.

The reason that I have presented this brief outline of my life during more than a quarter century is because you can find and adapt similar opportunities to your own personal life. I have made the guidelines for success, which follow, in the form of nine steps. Use them so that you may become prosperous and successful in whatever undertaking you favor.

I should answer in advance of the nine steps a question that may occur to you: Why should a chapter on prosperity (money) be in a book on how to be in touch with the power of the spirit? For the answer to this question, I call again on Brian Luke Seaward whose *Stand Like Mountain, Flow Like Water,* contains an informative

statement that gives to prosperity the blessing of the divine
will of the universe.

"The Law of Dharma states that everyone has a
unique purpose in life, which is manifested through those
inner resources that comprise our spiritual essence.
Universal in nature, this message can also be found in the
words of Jesus of Nazareth when he said, 'I come to serve,
not to be served.'

"When we utilize these gifts and share the fruits of our
work, we fulfill the divine will of the universe. In turn, we
experience the ecstasy and exhilaration of our own spirit.
That, too, is worthy of sharing. So our life purpose must
neither be concealed nor confined to a chosen few, but
nurtured, utilized and shared openly with all who may
benefit from our best efforts and achievements.

"There is a parable in the New Testament that speaks
to the nature of utilizing such gifts and talents.

"'A rich man called three of his finest workers to meet
with him before his trip to a land far away. Each was given
a large sum of money with directions to plan wisely so that
upon his return, he would reap the benefits of their investments. After entrusting each servant with a third of his
fortune, he reminded them that each would have to account
for their deeds.

"'Upon his return, the three men were summoned
individually into private consultation. In a short time he
learned that two of the three men invested wisely and
revealed a fourfold profit. The third servant, perhaps acting
out of fear, buried his cash for safekeeping, and thus earned
no interest on the capital. The master furiously admonished
his servant, and then imprisoned him for his foolishness.'

"I have to admit that whenever I heard this passage, I
found myself empathizing with the gentleman who buried

the money, perhaps because I was so incensed with the greed of his master. Furthermore, I thought, why was the Church advocating long-term financial investments? Does this have something to do with the collection plate?

"My thoughts on this issue closely parallel those of the late Joseph Campbell, who once said that we need to get rid of all banking terms when we discuss issues of spirituality. It wasn't until years later that I learned the words 'money' and 'talents' were often used interchangeably in biblical translations. The version of the New Testament I was exposed to obviously opted for the banking metaphor.

"Reflecting on this story now, the true message becomes crystal clear. The moral of this tale suggests that security comes from using our talents to their greater potential; this means sharing them with others. As far as the grounding process is concerned, if we conceal those mystical insights, those creative thoughts or that wisdom of divine consciousness, then we continue to remain locked into the confines of fear-based thinking. Ultimately, the perpetual stress feeds upon itself."

Briefly, Seaward tells us what Jesus and the Bible instructed, "Be prosperous and multiply." It is okay to be prosperous: "God loves a prosperous man."

Now, let's examine the Nine Steps.

Step One: To exercise your personal power of prosperity, you must keep an account of how you spend your money. Carry a small notebook in your pocket and write down everything you spend on a daily basis. Record how much you spend on groceries, food that you eat out and even incidentals like newspapers and magazines. At the end of the month add up, on a separate sheet, the totals under such headings as food, postage, car expenses, entertainment, health, personal, etc. To make sure that you account for every penny you spend, add up how much money you have in your pocket at the start of each day and how much you have left at the end of the day. This way you can keep an accurate account of what you spend. Also, list what you spend each month when you write checks for the electricity bill, telephone, insurance, taxes and items listed on your credit cards. Then, at the end of the year, make a final balance sheet. You don't need to do this every year. I personally do it every fourth or fifth year just to check on my spending habits.

Next, look to see what you pay out on expendable goods such as food, entertainment and vacations, in which case, it seems that you have nothing to show for the money spent. Also list your capital expenditure for cars, furniture, appliances and other durable goods, which last long enough to prove that you have something for your money in years to come. Finally, list the money spent on items that you did not really need in the first place or never used. You might say to yourself, I don't want to spend that much time going into detail over my monetary expenditures. To this observation, you might acknowledge that there are very few people who exercise the time and energy to become prosperous. If prosperity is your goal, you should do it.

Step Two: Make a budget and prepare to plan for the future. Decide that from this point forward you will set aside your budgeted amount of money for your expenses. Be honest with yourself and decide what expenditures you can do without. Find out what you can live on and how much money would be sufficient for all your needs. You can always live on less. Most people overestimate their needs. I am not suggesting that you do without sufficient food and clothing, but you must live within the size of your income. Make a sensible budget and live within certain boundaries.

These are vital steps you should take if you are serious about becoming prosperous.

Step Three: The importance of living within your means is the way to prosperity. My father told me something when I was a little boy which I have never forgotten and, in fact, I still practice it to this very day. He said, "If you earn ten English pounds a week and only spend nine pounds, nineteen shillings and eleven pence, you will be a happy person. However, if you spend ten pounds and one penny, you will be an unhappy person." It is absolutely essential not to spend one penny more than you earn; even if it means going without certain pleasures. If you get into debt, you create problems for yourself. Your debts will literally become your enemies.

Credit cards are a way of life in this modern world. Credit cards encourage you and make it easy for you to spend money that you don't have. Credit cards are a scourge in present times. Latest figures show the average American householder owes $7,000 in credit card debt. Personally, I carry one credit card, which I need when traveling, especially in foreign countries where your cash may not be accepted. I pay off my credit card at the end of each month. Recently, I was away so long that one month I was not at home to pay off the charges on my credit card. When I returned home and received my next statement, I found a "Thank you" message printed on my bill. Why? Because the company was now able to charge me interest on my unpaid bill. The company won and I lost. Credit cards create higher prices. If you must use a credit card, make sure that you settle your account on a monthly basis. Now, if you want to join that elite group of people who make money and become financially successful, that five percent of the population who can retire in comfort, recognize the monetary facts of life. If you borrow unnecessarily and pay interest for the privilege, you will find that you have a hole in your pocket. Learn to live within your means. Never spend more than you earn. It may take discipline to curb the thirst to spend, but the results of budgeted spending will pay off in the long run. This is a great way to build up your savings for a rainy day or to be able to put a down payment on a house.

Step Four: You should divide up your income into four distinct divisions. Yours to use is the sum left after you have paid your taxes (Render unto Caesar what is Caesar's). Then divide the balance in the following manner: seventy, ten, ten, ten. This is a well tried and proven system. I use this concept and so can you, simply because it works.

The seventy percent is used to pay for your daily living expenses, all those items that you have recorded in your notebook. In other words, you decide that you will now live on seventy cents of every dollar earned after taxes. The first ten percent becomes your savings account. You continue to save and accumulate money until you have sufficient cash to be able to make a down payment on a house or buy a car or any other large ticket item. The second ten percent you use for your life insurance, IRA's and retirement funds. The third ten percent you set aside for your favorite charity and share with others less fortunate. This step number four of dividing everything you earn into four clear cut divisions will lead you in the direction of prosperity.

Step Five: This deals with that first sum of money, the seventy percent. From this amount you pay for your food, clothing, housing and the basic needs of life. Notice that I refer to your needs, not your wants. The basic needs of life are items that you need for survival — food, clothes, heat, light, telephone, rent and transportation. The wants of

life are the luxury items like cameras, camcorders, elec-
trical gadgets, fashion name-brand clothes, eating out in
restaurants, alcoholic beverages, cigarettes and expensive
vacations, and the list goes on. Unfortunately, most people
not only don't keep within the limits of using seventy
percent of their earning for their needs, but they spend not
only one hundred percent of their earnings, but even
borrow money to pay for their excess spending habits.
They use credit cards, take out loans and saddle themselves
with payments they can ill afford. Now, if you want to be
financially independent, that means you must not borrow
from other people. Being financially independent means
just that, being independent, using only your own money
and not other people's money. In the western world, where
we have so much in the way of material goods, it should
not be too difficult for any one of us to make do with less.
I travel the world and see how the majority of people have
so little. Surely, it is okay to tighten your purse strings,
especially in the early part of your life, so that you may
reap the rewards of carefully planned spending when you
are older.

Step Six: Next, take your first ten percent of everything that you earn after taxes and create a savings fund, so
that as early in life as possible, you can save enough money
to purchase your own home. Take out a mortgage, which is
secured by your down payment and make a monthly
mortgage payment instead of paying rent. When you rent,
you have nothing to show for your money. If you pay rent,
guess who is becoming more prosperous? It is the person to
whom you pay the rent, certainly not you. However, when
you slowly but surely make your mortgage payments, you
are building equity and your capital wealth automatically
increases. To go from paying monthly rent to paying a

monthly mortgage is a great step forward to exercising your power to become prosperous.

I personally have never bought a new house. I prefer to buy an older building that needs repairs and repainting. The house not only costs less in the first place but after you have fixed it up, it will be worth more within a year's time than what you originally paid for it. That's fast appreciation. The lower the cost when you buy, the lower the down payment and monthly mortgage payments. Financially, a fifteen-year mortgage works better than a thirty-year mortgage. Not only do you pay the mortgage off in half the time, but you pay overall less money in interest.

The country of Singapore enforces an automatic savings plan upon its citizens. The government of Singapore withholds a percentage of a worker's wages, which is set aside in a savings account. This saved money can only be withdrawn when the worker has enough to negotiate buying a large ticket item such as a car or a house. More people in Singapore own their homes than any other country in the world. Now, in this country of America, you have to learn to discipline yourself to save ten percent of your income for a down payment on a house. Maybe it is a little harder to do this, but you have the freedom to do it your own way.

Finally, when you have saved sufficient funds to become the proud owner of your own home, you can continue saving ten percent. These savings can be placed in an investment of your own choice. It is not my place to advise on stocks and bonds. If you want advice, consult a person who has already demonstrated success with his own money on the stock market. However, I would suggest that it is best to invest in funds that are growth oriented and also consider letting any earned interest compound on a monthly basis. Let your money grow for you. Money makes money and leads to prosperity.

Step Seven: The second ten percent of your earnings, after paying taxes, should be set aside for your retirement years and old age. You need to invest in a life insurance policy to take care of a spouse or any dependents that look to you for sustenance. Place money, on a regular basis, into a pension-type fund. There are many from which you can choose. Perhaps you could take out an annuity, preferably the deferred type that you don't draw upon until you really need the income. As good as it may be to take advice from other people in monetary matters, including financial advisers, above all, listen to your own hunches and intuition.

Saving for the years to come is like saving for a rainy day. I was brought up in England as a child and my parents were very thrifty. So when World War II started in September 1939, my mother had a year's supply of food stored away and my father had accumulated several tons of solid fuel in the form of coal and anthracite for the hot water boiler that heated our house. Thus, our family lived well in the early part of the war at the time of national food and fuel shortages. From the wisdom of my parents, I have always learned to be prepared for hard times. I have, personally, over a period of years, accumulated a reserve fund of money in the form of a healthy bank balance on my current account, as well as cash in a savings account and a few gold and silver coins that I have hidden away. In other words, I have enough solvent funds so that if I couldn't earn any money, I could continue to live comfortably for a couple of years or so, without having to do a day's work. I sincerely advise you to take steps to protect yourself and your family against hard times and whatever emergency may arise. I have some canned and dried food in reserve. I even have candles and lamp oil stored away in case of electricity cuts. I keep diesel oil in drums for my diesel car and tractor should there ever be a fuel shortage. It is so much better to be safe than sorry.

Step Eight: The third ten percent is to be put aside to assist other people, especially those less fortunate than yourself or people who have a crisis to handle. Maybe you are a person who already tithes ten percent of your earnings consistently on a monthly basis to a particular charity; that is great. I myself have never tithed, I prefer to keep cash available to give help when needed and in a way that touches my heart. One of the things that I enjoy doing is supporting a young child in India through an organization called Childreach. The money that I provide ensures that he will have enough to eat and gain a basic education. This boy has indicated that he wants to become a teacher so if possible, I will help him attain a college education. As I have grown older in years, I have come to realize that we are all interdependent on each other. Rather than say I have to be financially independent, I prefer to say that I need to become financially interdependent. I desire to work with other people like you, rather than separate myself from you. My whole philosophy of life is that I take my talent, which in my particular case is teaching, and make this, my gift, available to you and others out there in the world at large. I am aware that to the degree that I serve my fellow human beings, so does the world reward and look after me. This third ten percent of my income, as far as I am concerned, becomes a very important investment, which I share with other people who need help. Since we are all one large family on planet Earth, we really need to share our prosperity openly with each other.

Step Nine: Learn to be cash conscious. For example, check your checkbook. Keep a record of the checks that you write. Maintain a running balance so that you know exactly how much cash you have on current account on any particular day. My monthly bank statement comes a few days prior to the end of the month so I don't write any checks for about one week or so prior to this time. This way, when my bank statement arrives, I can check to see how accurate I have been in keeping my records in order. It is a personal challenge to me to make sure I balance my checkbook to the exact penny. I have done this for years. I get very upset with myself if I am even one penny off in my calculations. It should be important to you to know exactly where you stand. Keeping your checkbook in order is an aid to prosperity.

It is also a good policy to count the money that you have on your person at the beginning of each day and again when you empty your pockets or purse at night. This keeps you aware of what you spend on a daily basis. Learn to become more cash conscious. The more that you know about how much you have, the less likely you are to squander your money. Be proud that you have your finances under control. People often laugh at the way I take so much trouble to look after my cash, but the last laugh is with me because I have lived for well over seventy years and I have never been broke or busted. I have been financially successful in every venture that I have undertaken including the founding of two private schools, operating a restaurant, founding and teaching Mind Dynamics and, more recently, Inward Bound. I have always had enough money to live comfortably. Some would say I have been lucky, but I notice that "good luck" follows those who work hard and pay attention to their finances. Therefore, develop a good work ethic, take responsibility for yourself, help others and above all, look after your cash as outlined in these nine steps. God only helps those who help themselves.

The symbol for your ninth personal power of prosperity is a three-sided triangular pyramid. Nine is the triple three and each of the three triangles has three sides which come to nine. The first triangle is the law of creation as discussed in Chapter Three. The male, love energy interacts with the female, intuitive life to create the result — the child, the light. "Let love move through your life so that you may be a light to the world." The second triangle is the power of action and work to manifest at the objective physical level, as demonstrated in Chapter Six. The third triangle represents the money and prosperity that you attain by using the subjective power to manifest objectively the results that you desire. All action and work receives its rewards, especially when you put into action these nine steps to achieve prosperity. These nine steps represent what you do physically to become prosperous. However, Chapter Four explained the four different body levels at which you can function: physical, emotional, mental and spiritual. Likewise, you can use your power to prosper in four distinct ways.

The *physical* level: Work for a living. Exert physical energy to earn money to pay for your needs and follow the nine steps enumerated earlier in this chapter.

The *emotional* level comes after the physical level of operation. How do you become prosperous emotionally? You add feeling and enthusiasm to the nine steps just outlined. You put to good use your emotional energy. You have "faith" in what you do. A simple definition of faith that I learned in Sunday School is, "Father And I Together Here: F-A-I-T-H." When you have faith in a higher source, such as Father God energy, then you know for sure that prosperity is assured. You might say to yourself, "It is hard for me to accept this." Think back to when you were a child and had faith in your parental father to provide your daily needs, such as food to eat, clothes to wear and a bed to sleep in. Then, just transform this faith from your earthly father to your heavenly, spiritual Father God. Have faith on your road to prosperity. If you bank with and on God, you will never be broke or busted.

The *mental* level comes next. Use the greatest creative part of your mind, your power to image. Create a picture in great detail in your mind of how you want to prosper. Don't put numbers and dollar signs in your picture. Just imagine the end results, the items that you wish to have, do not put a monetary amount on their worth. God does not think in numbers. The picture that you image is like a magnetic force field that arranges physical matter into the end products that you desire. "What you image is what you get." So imagine yourself being prosperous the way you want to be.

The *spiritual* level comes last, but is far from being the least. When you are aware spiritually, you realize you already have everything. At this spiritual level you are able to perceive oneness and merge yourself into the oneness of all life. Your spiritual self does not experience lack because it already has everything. You evoke and call out from your spiritual self all that already exists within, which is the opposite from the first three steps. How do your draw out this inner wealth so that you can prosper? You simply practice the art of giving. Let your spiritual self express itself by giving to and serving others as explained in step number eight and also in Chapter Eight. It has been said that "Prosperity needs to circulate through your affairs as air circulates through your lungs." You know that fresh new air can't enter your lungs unless the existing air is first exhaled. Likewise, you can't inhale and become prosperous unless you learn the art of exhaling and giving of your substance. If you desire to prosper spiritually, you must be one with your spiritual self. Jesus said, as recorded in the Bible, "Seek first the kingdom of heaven and all will be added unto you." Accept your links with God by being conscious of your spiritual self. You will then reap the inevitable rewards and become prosperous. Realize you already have. Be aware of the oneness of life. Be one with God. Just be. Be a center for evocation. Be a co-creator with God. To the degree that you know who you are spiritually, so will you manifest all that you need. The best way to act is to use all four body levels.

Spiritually — accept that you already are prosperous.

Mentally — image prosperity in the form of a picture.

Emotionally — have faith that you will manifest prosperity.

Physically — use the nine steps listed in this chapter.

Be active and serve. God only helps those who help themselves. With all this information concerning how to use your four body levels — physical, emotional, mental and spiritual — together with the nine practical steps on how to deal with your finances, I am certain that you will prosper not only in your own eyes but in those loftier ones that inspire the beauty of the world.

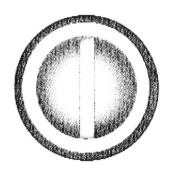

Chapter Ten

Centering

Meditational exercises will help you to experience perfected selflessness leading to peace and happiness.

Buddha

By now you have learned that my role in life is that of a teacher. I am here to show people how to enter a higher state. It is all a matter of becoming more aware of the genius within, developing and using it. We tend to look to powers outside ourselves. I want people to look within. Hence, the title of the book you are reading, *Inward Bound,* is also the name I give to my seminar.

In this chapter I am going to describe the simple, but marvelous process of centering the self. The purpose is to make a reunion with our real selves — to touch upon the magnificence of who we are.

This journey inward, which I demonstrate in this chapter, is paralleled in the mystical tradition by the observations by historical mystics that ordinary human nature opens into vast inner worlds. Various metaphors have illustrated this fact of spiritual life. In the Greek myth of the Minotaur, the path to transformation led through the labyrinth; the seeker, like Theseus, had to find his way with the help of Ariadne's golden thread, which symbolized a teacher's leading — as I hope to lead you. The soul has been pictured as a mansion [Saint Teresa's "interior castle"] or as a Magic Theatre [in Herman Hesse's *Steppenwolf]*, in which one space opens into many others. Hindu and Buddhist writings describe a multitude of inner worlds. As Sri Aurobindo writes, "We have not learned to distinguish the different parts of our being; for these are usually lumped together simply as 'mind'.... Therefore [we] do not understand our own states and actions...."

Speaking of inner worlds, one Christian mystic, an unnamed monk wrote, a book probably about the fourteenth century entitled *The Cloud of Unknowing.* It promised advice for all persons desiring "to be knit to God in Spirit, in unity of love, and accordance of will."

According to Herbert Benson who wrote *The Relaxation Response,* the anonymous monk who penned the book kept his identity secret because he feared he would be accused of heresy. "He believed," Benson wrote, "religion allowed for independent inquiry and individual experience, which at that time were condemned by the church. In his book he wrote that man gained direct knowledge of God by losing all awareness of himself. Referring to his title, the author depicts a passive attitude as the way 'to cover,' or forget, all distractions.

"'Try to cover these thoughts with a thick cloud of forgetting as though they never existed neither for you nor for any other man. And if they continue to arise, continue to put them down.'

"He goes on to discuss the element of 'dwelling upon' and advises that his readers can develop 'special ways, tricks, private techniques, and spiritual devices' in order to achieve contemplation. One means is the use of a single syllable such as 'God' or 'love':

"'Choose whichever one you prefer, or if you like, choose another that suits your tastes, provided that it is of one syllable. And clasp this word tightly in your heart so that it never leaves it no matter what may happen. This word shall be your shield and your spear whether you ride in peace or in war. With this word you shall beat upon the cloud and the darkness, which are above you. With this word you shall strike down thoughts of every kind and drive them beneath the cloud of forgetting.'"

A number of mystics rose in Germany during the fourteenth century. As in *The Cloud of Unknowing,* the base of their mysticism was the belief that the individual could directly commune with God when he was in a state of perfect solitude.

Among those searchers for the dwelling place of the universal spirit was Martin Luther, who drew upon this doctrine of individual transcendence to God. Rudolph Otto, a prominent German theologian and philosopher, described methods of prayer from Luther's book *How Man Should Pray, Meister Peter, the Barber,* written in 1534, Luther say: "To prepare for prayers of inward recollections, the true language of the heart, in which one concentrates solely upon God, one must achieve a passive attitude by dwelling upon an object. It is necessary to have 'the heart free itself and become joyous' in order to prevent thoughts from intruding."

To create the appropriate mindset for concentration, Luther suggests the words of the Lord's Prayer, the Ten Commandments, the Psalms, or a number of the sayings of Christ or Paul.

But it is Larry Dossey, author of *Recovering the Soul* who points out with remarkable insight and clarity that the "[mental constructs] we make of mysticism are at once illogical:

"Mysticism — the word itself conjures images of distant times and distant places; temple bells and gongs; rare incense; weathered texts and interminable solitude; meditation and asceticism. Yet these mental constructs we make of mysticism are at once illogical — for if the goal of the mystic is union with reality, there is nothing on the surface which would necessarily localize such a goal to distant climes or to obscure places, since, surely, "reality" transcends such relativities. We would expect reality, whatever it is, to be unaffected by such cultural phenomena as saffron robes and alms bowls, or we shouldn't call it 'reality' at all. Reality, we feel, is encompassing. As Yung-chia Ta-Shih states, 'There is one Nature and one reality. It belongs to no particular culture, to no particular time.'

"This is worth remembering, worth saying to ourselves over and over, for the reason that some of the most profound commentaries about the mystical ideals of oneness and unity that have ever surfaced in the history of human thought are contemporary. This discovery comes as a shock to those who prefer their mysticism flavored with cultural artifacts and ancient traditions. And yet it is a lesson the great adepts of the mystical way would have us learn early on: it is in our own back yard, our own time, our own self that truth lies; we need not look elsewhere."

Of course, Dossey is perfectly correct. It is the "inner life" I seek to explore when I lead spiritual aspirants through the process of getting in touch with the everlasting reality inside themselves, and it is the discovery of how to become inward bound that is the whole purpose of this book. Those who have become inward bound, inner-directed, able to see with less cloudy vision into their own futures, find purpose in their lives and a sense of the grand continuity beyond the body. They may experience the exuberant, expansive, smiling-all-over feeling listeners feel when they hear Barbra Streisand sing, "On a clear day, rise and look around you, and see who you are...."

The answer to who we are is the fascinating definition most of us seek. Those of us who find the path to the inner life become expanded humans, whose direction becomes more accurate, whose vision becomes more far reaching.

How does one commence the process of self exploration?

This is a common question and the answer may seem obvious. The body is the centering point, the place to start from which to reach beyond, to flesh out the spirit with the grace of understanding our purpose. Once we understand our purpose, why we are here on planet Earth, then our individual lives make more sense. We no longer have to stumble through life as if we were wearing blinders. We can become successful people with marvelous futures that extend beyond our limited vision.

I wrote about purpose in the first chapter of this book, but the fact is the whole idea of human purpose requires defining and redefining as we take longer and longer steps into the future of understanding. But many people never stop to think about the question of purpose, or "why do anything in life that's worthwhile?" But there is only one unchangeable answer to the question, What is the purpose of life? Around 500 B.C., Socrates put it in two words, which he had carved above the entrance to his academy: Know Thyself. The whole purpose of life is to know who we are. If we did, we would never be sick, never be poor, never have a bad relationship; we would have the right job, be happy and prosperous. When we get in touch with the power within, we know we are part of God. The whole of God is indivisible and is within you.

I like to think of this idea as God being an ocean. You go out in a boat, and for thousands of miles there is ocean. But you can lean over the side and scoop up some of the water with a glass or cup. Now you have sea water that has everything in it that the whole ocean has. Even in one drop of ocean water, everything is in it.

You're like a glass full of God's ocean. Within that glass you represent everything that's there. You are complete and whole.

And yet we do not believe it. In response to an awakening soul power in us we attend seminars looking for a list of ingredients in our glass of water. We attend lectures, go to churches, read books and talk to people. And according to how deeply we seek, so do we find. But the key to understanding is that we must allow what we find to become a part of our consciousness. There are millions of seekers; there are a few thousand finders. Only about ten percent of the finders actually realize what they have and how effective they can be.

The spirituality of which I speak can be known by any person directly through deliberate practices such as prayer

or centering the self, because we are secretly joined with the
Everlasting already. What we must do is to remove the veil
from our eyes. Centering is but one of the techniques.

I think it might be worthwhile to examine what one
great thinker's view of spiritual reality is. I'm referring to
the late Carl Jung, psychiatrist, writer, philosopher, who
was never so certain than when he asserted that paying
attention to the manifestations of the timeless Mind was the
redeeming life task for all persons. This task is especially
difficult in our era because we have shifted all emphasis to
the here and now — to doing, to consuming, to practicality,
to material progress. But, as Jung clearly believed, the One
Mind cannot be put in a box in the here-and-now because it
is infinite and eternal. And because its concept of space and
time is different from that which we commonly value, we
find ourselves cut off from it. The result has been
predictable: We have become victims of our own unconscious drives, and a materialization of our world has come
about. But our task in life is just the reverse, Jung insists:
"The exact opposite: to become conscious of the contents
that press upward from the unconscious" — to "create," as
he put it, "more and more consciousness." Only in this way
can we realize "the sole purpose of human existence: ... to
kindle a light in the darkness of mere being."

Jung, and other enlightened philosophers who
followed in the footsteps of his beliefs, did not agree with
the tendency of the Western religions to regard the soul as
something small, ignominious, unworthy, personal, and
subjective. He pointed out the contradictions of this view by
questioning how could something so small and unworthy be
immortal? — as all of the religions from centuries back
insist. All around us, he said, there are clues to the contrary
— that the soul is magnificently unbounded — and he spent

a lifetime accumulating evidence for this. His conclusion: "The soul is assuredly not small, but the radiant Godhead itself."

The connection between the soul and consciousness? Jung came to the conclusion that human consciousness is "the invisible, intangible manifestation of the soul." Thus the task of "creating more and more consciousness" (meaning an expansion of the awareness of the infinity of the God-self) becomes the equivalent of recovering the soul and regaining contact with the inner divinity. But how can this be done?

How can we regain contact with the inner divinity? One answer comes from centering. The centering technique brings about several direct benefits as a result of aligning the body with the spirit.

Seven Major Benefits

1. When we center, we create better health by freeing our intuition to tell us how we need to improve our immune systems. This means exercising properly, eating correctly and doing what we should to keep our bodies strong. We are constantly exposed to germs and diseases. When the immune system is in balance, we are able to ward off illness. If we are centered and feel good about ourselves, we cannot think ourselves ill. We are not going to psychosomatically make ourselves unhealthy. Centering allows us to align with our inner power to stay physically fit.

2. When we learn to center ourselves and go within, we relax. When we relax, there is less stress and it is

very easy to get more restful sleep anywhere and at any time.

3.   Another benefit of centering is the release of more happiness. Happiness is not something we receive later in life when we retire. It is a means of traveling; a way of life. When we center, we see what we need to do in life. And happiness is fulfilling our purpose.

4.   Longer life is another benefit of centering. Man is actually designed to live one hundred twenty years, not the seventy we are accustomed to thinking about. We are programmed to work until we are sixty or sixty-five, then we retire, and five years later we die. But if we program ourselves differently, we can choose our own life spans.

5.   Among the nice things that happen to people who are centered is the appearance of more friends in their lives. When we center ourselves and get in touch with who we are, have better health and are more relaxed and happy, others will want to be around us. People relate to what we are — our demeanor, our beingness, our charisma — not to what we say. If we are centered, people will be attracted to us like moths to a candle. Those around us will want to be with us and share with us because we are at one with our inner power.

6.   Another direct benefit of centering is that the individual becomes less accident prone. If we are centered, we are more aware of what is going on around us. Minor awkwardness, such as knocking over a glass of water, or a major automobile accident can be avoided when we are aware of our surroundings. If we are aware, we will move the

glass of water or get out of the way of the person driving foolishly.

You see, there really are no accidents in life. They are self-created. You can learn not to create them by being centered and aware.

7. For persons to whom wealth is important, centering bestows the benefit of more money. When we know our purpose in life, when our work fulfills our unique talent so that we have pleasure in accomplishing our daily tasks, we will be productive, successful and we will make more money. We are paid in direct proportion to what we give, and when we are centered and feel good about what we are doing, we give openly and generously to the world.

If you say, "I want to be a millionaire!" do you know what you have to do? Just give one million dollars worth of service and share yourself in a way whereby you are giving one million dollars. Then you will get what you want.

Don't try to find a quick way to make money, because you will lose it. Oh, you might make it, I'm not saying you won't. But it will not stay with you. The way to make money and to keep it flowing is to have the consciousness of the fact that you are here to serve.

Further Benefits

Evidence of the power of centering to produce marked changes in the body is becoming more widespread. For example, in 1975, the physician Herbert Benson proposed in his best-selling book, *The Relaxation Response,* that by practicing a simple form of meditation (similar but not quite the same as centering), a person can change his heart rate, respiration and brain waves. They slow down with meditation, muscles relax, and the effects of epinephrine and other stress-related hormones diminish. Studies have shown that by routinely seeking "the relaxation response" (by centering or meditating), seventy-five percent of insomniacs begin to sleep normally. Many women who have been infertile become pregnant, and chronic pain sufferers in about thirty-four percent of the cases reduce their use of painkilling drugs.

In his latest book, *Timeless Healing,* Benson points out that prayer operates along the same chemical pathways as the relaxation response, providing the power to affect corticosteroid messengers in the body, or "stress hormones," leading to lower blood pressure, more relaxed heart rate and respiration, and other benefits. So does centering, for it embraces the same meditative process of letting go.

According to one authority, David Felton, chairman of the Department of Neurobiology at the University of Rochester, quoted in a *Time* magazine article on faith and healing, "Anything involved with meditation and controlling the state of mind that alters hormone activity has the potential to have an impact on the immune system."

There is no question but that centering on a regular basis not only brings the physiological benefits of the "relaxation response," but it provides the qualitative mindset for solving life's vexing problems with greater personal equanimity.

We all need to center every day for at least fifteen minutes. If we do just fifteen minutes per day, the balance of the twenty-four hours will be much more in harmony.

The best time to center is early in the morning. Perhaps you like to do your chores first — tend to the cat and dog, brush your teeth and so forth — or perhaps you like to center when you first get out of bed. Sit near an open window, burn incense, light a candle, have flowers near by. Create your own magic.

Based on information concerning the physical posture most conducive to centering, it seems more natural for us as Westerners to sit in a chair with our feet flat on the floor. If you want to take your shoes off, do so. Arms and legs should be uncrossed. You can sit on the floor, but make sure your spine is straight—and your back is against the wall. The energy flows through the base of the spine upwards, and if the spine has a kink in it, the energy is obstructed.

The peace and quiet that you can find in the centering process comes about as a result of stilling your body. To enter the fourth state of consciousness, you have to still the body, still the emotions, still the mind, to enter the place where peace is.

The following explanation of the centering technique is based on utilizing the seven colors of the rainbow.

When a white light passes through a prism, the seven colors of the rainbow are formed. These represent the seven aspects of God. The Old Testament calls it the Elohim God, which are the seven rays of Elohe or God. God comes at seven levels, and He awakens our bodies at seven points. In India, these points are called chakras. The chakras and the colors of the rainbow help activate the highest part of us.

The lowest part is the color red, located on the outermost band of the rainbow. The highest is violet, the innermost color. So we go from red to violet to reach our innermost part of being. Red represents the physical part, the external. The next color, orange, is the emotional part, the color expressing feeling. Yellow symbolizes the mental. The fourth color is green, the color of peace. In order to reach the green peaceful state, you have to quiet the red physical part of you, calm the orange emotional part, and still the yellow mental part so that you can enter the fourth spiritual state.

The fifth color is blue, which represents love. Purple is the mental level of spirituality—the knowing level of the masters. Violet represents the spiritual-spiritual, where consciousness becomes one with God.

All of the colors are psychological trigger devices, a method to bring you peace by centering yourself. Centering is not the only method of coming to peace, of course. It is the one I use, because I wanted to find something that did not clash with Buddhism, Hinduism, Christianity, Judaism or any religion. Every religion will accept the colors of the rainbow. Every religion will accept nature. I have tried to create a universal spiritual language.

The Centering Procedure

Now, you can begin the actual steps of centering yourself. You start with the color red and progress, as you move deeper into yourself, to the color violet.

Following is a step-by-step explanation of the centering procedure that will take you inward bound:

First, close your eyes and visualize the seven colors of the rainbow. You might wish to create a rainbow in your mind's eye and imagine yourself passing from the outside band of red inward toward violet. Slowly, as if you were a traveler on a quiet journey of self-discovery, pass through red, orange, yellow, green. Depending on your visualization powers, you may actually see the different colors vividly as you progress through the rainbow stages. Your passage should be slow and silent, free of mind clatter and interruptions. Start your centering exercise by saying to yourself:

I now prepare to center myself. The first color I will visualize is red. I will actually see the color red in my mind, and in sequence as I progress, I will visualize the other colors of the rainbow.

Red:

I first will visualize the color red. I relax my body from head to foot. I relax, let go of my body. Relax.

When you release the muscles around the eyes, the throat area and the lungs, the rest of the body will let go.

Orange:

I next visualize the color orange. I release and let go of all of my emotions. I desire only that which is good for others.

To forget yourself and your desires, direct your energy into the desire to help others. Put aside your own desires and say,

I want to help my fellow man the best way I can.

When you do this, your personal desires and needs become less.

Yellow:

I calm and still my mind, I bring my mind to rest.

This is the statement you say to yourself. To still the mind, see yourself somewhere in nature — in a park, by a river, in the desert, in a garden — wherever it is natural for you to be. When the mind is surrounded by nature, your thinking slows down, you become more peaceful.

Green:

I allow peace to come into my life. I sense a state of peacefulness within every cell of my body.

Now you can enter peace: you have stilled your body, stilled the emotions and stilled the mind.

Blue:

I let love permeate my entire being. I feel myself full of love.

Many people cannot love because they are not at peace. How can you love when you are upset physically, emotionally and mentally? Note that peace, the green color, comes before love, the blue color.

Purple:

I seek out the depths within. I aspire to that inner secret place.

Purple is the master level of accepting and knowing who you are. When you are peaceful and loving, you then desire the very highest, you aspire to that which is beyond.

Violet:

I enter the inner-most part of my being. I am now there. I am centered.

The whole purpose of life is to know who you are, that you are of God and to return to that knowledge. And you do it by following the seven steps of the rainbow. You do this by releasing your body, releasing your emotions, and releasing your mind; entering a peaceful state, loving of others, desiring oneness with God. This is a natural sequence; you become centered.

In the last stage of being centered you say to yourself:

I am now one with my inner-self, a state which
encompasses all of time, so that I just become aware
of the totality of the now. I am only conscious of the
present. I feel and sense this one moment in time ...
I just realize myself right now.

We live in a three dimensional world that tells us there is yesterday, today and tomorrow. But when we are centered, we enter the spiritual realm and the only time is now. Reality is that there is no yesterday and there is no tomorrow. There is only the now.

The only way I can illustrate that there is only "the now" is with an analogy.

If you look through a keyhole into a room, you don't see very much. Keyholes are very narrow. Imagine that you're looking through a keyhole and somebody walks across the room. You won't see where he has come from; you won't see where he is going. You only see when he crosses that little viewpoint you have of looking through the keyhole.

Now, what would you physically do to see that person walk across the room? You'd open the door! And you'd see the whole trip.

Most have the narrow consciousness of the keyhole. They don't know what has happened or what's going to happen. All they see is now and that might not look too good.

When you grow in consciousness, you open the door of your consciousness. You see everything. You see what's happened, what's happening and what's going to happen.

When you center yourself, that will take place. You will have a greater awareness and consciousness than you have right now.

The Experience of Centering

"I will experience whatever I'm led to experience." At this moment you should be open to receive, to hear inner guidance. When you feel most at peace, relaxed, with your heart, mind, with your whole body, open and welcoming to the universe, you are truly centered. Your soul is laid bare and open enough so that it can manifest whatever it is that you need in your life at this time. This is not a time to ask for anything. Just use it for a time to be open to hear the inner voice. If you want, you can always ask an open-ended question. You can say to yourself as you center, "Where should I go in life?" "What should I do?" and then listen to the intuition guiding you and showing you the way.

There is one thing you must not do. You must not say, "I want this, or I'm going to have that, and I'm going to make it happen through centering." That is not what the process is about. The process is meant to encourage the intuition to guide you where you want to go. Guidance may come in any number of ways; a voice, a vision or a feeling.

Evaluating the Centering Experience

What happens during the "now" of the centering experience? Will you see visions? What comes to people who have led their minds into a restful, open, receptive state?

Dozens of people I have talked with describe their ascent through a long tunnel which leads them toward a dim

light that often becomes brighter. It is a peaceful voyage up
the tunnel toward the promising brightness. Some people
have told me they have gone beyond the tunnel into an area
where they have dimly perceived saintly, gentle figures who
welcome the seeker with beckoning arms. The tunnel with
the dim light at the end seems to be a more common experience during centering. Others experience no sense of
traveling or ascending; they describe a feeling of being
totally connected to everything in their world — a oneness
with all life and all things which the creator has provided.
But whatever the nature of the vision, indisputably people
return from centering refreshed, shed of worries, clean of
unworthy thoughts, relieved of the clamors of the day,
feeling more as an integrated part of everything that is.

The more you practice centering, the more effective
you will become as a human and the more you will appreciate the growing awareness in your self that you are a
marvelous, unfolding mystery within The Great Mystery,
and that you have the power to make anything of your life
that you wish.

Of course, there have been reports of remarkable
centering experiences which are more specific in content
and which reflect the higher degrees of consciousness that
can be reached through unusual circumstances. Such a one
was described by Charles Lindbergh in his book, *The Spirit
of St. Louis*. It happened to him during his epic flight to
Paris. All the conditions for centering were present as he sat
alone in his plane almost adrift from his body:

"While I'm staring at the instruments, during an
unearthly age of time, both conscious and asleep, the
fuselage behind becomes filled with ghostly presences —
vaguely outlined forms, transparent, moving, riding weight-
less with me in the plane. I feel no surprise at their coming.

There is no suddenness to their appearance. Without turning my head, I see them as clearly as though in my normal field of vision. There's no limit to my sight — my skull is one great eye, seeing everywhere at once....

"All sense of substance leaves. There's no longer weight to my body, no longer hardness to the stick. The feeling of flesh is gone. I become independent of physical laws — of food, of shelter, of life. I'm almost one with these vapor-like forms behind me, less tangible than air, universal as ether. I'm still attached to life; they, not at all; but at any moment some thin band may snap and there will be no difference between us....

"I'm on the borderline of life and a greater realm beyond, as though caught in the field of gravitation between two planets, acted on by forces I can't control, forces too weak to be measured by any means at my command, yet representing powers incomparably stronger than I've ever known....

"Death no longer seems the final end it used to be, but rather the entrance to a new and free existence which includes all space, all time.

"Am I now more man or spirit? Will I fly my airplane on to Europe and live in flesh as I have before, feeling hunger, pain, and cold, or am I about to join these ghostly forms, become a consciousness in space, all-seeing, all-knowing, unhampered by the materialistic fetters of the world?"

From his moving experience, Lindbergh, like other men and women who have glimpsed "beyond the veil," was changed forever. He became a subtly different person.

Centering, as I have said before, is basically a form of meditation of which there are many expressions, as mountaineer Frank Smythe demonstrated in this statement from his book, *Mountain Vision:* "Physically you may feel but a cosmic speck of chemicalized dust, but spiritually you will feel great. For is not your vision capable in one glance of piercing the abysses of space? Is not your hearing attuned to an immortal harmony?..."

At the conclusion of your centering experience you may exit the fourth state of consciousness by ascending up through the spiritual energy levels from violet to red — traveling in reverse — going through the rainbow in the return sequence: Violet, purple, blue, green, yellow, orange and finally red. You move from the inner oneness to the outer physical state.

How long will centering take to work?

According to my experience and that of other spiritual masters I know, experiments show that it takes about 21 days to create a habit. Mark your calendar for twenty-one days and make sure — if need be enforce it on yourself — to center every day. After the three weeks, you really do not have to think about doing it anymore; it will have become automatic.

You are probably thinking: "All right, I do it for twenty-one days, it becomes automatic, I've created a habit. How long do I have to do it before I really see results in my life?"

The answer varies with the individual: It cannot be said that within three months or six months or nine months you will see incredible changes. It is like exercising: The first week is the hardest, then it gets easier and easier. But you don't really see changes in your body for several months. Some people see results almost immediately; others take almost a year.

Suppose you don't center yourself every day? Suppose you forget?

Missing a day or two is not going to invalidate the efforts you've put forth. I'd like for you think about how you drive your car. You have a steering wheel, and if you take your hands off of it, you may end up in a ditch. So you constantly have to make corrections. If you go off a little, just come back. The same applies when you're centering. If you get off course and take your hands off the wheel, so to speak, and quit doing it, what you've got to do is to take hold of the steering wheel again and direct yourself where you want to go — and that is to center on a daily basis.

The symbol for Chapter Ten, which is Centering consists of a circle which represents oneness and the upright one in the center represents you. So when you are centered you are in a state of oneness.

A full version of the centering procedure is printed in Appendix B.

Chapter
Eleven

Relationships

Let there be spaces in your togetherness.
Let the winds of heaven dance between you.

Kahlil Gibran

Your eleventh personal power is the power to relate so that you may have an ongoing relationship with another person. This relationship, when it is with someone of the opposite sex, ideally leads to a happy and lasting marriage. However, there are many other kinds of relationships, one such as that between parent and child. The topic of relationships in general is of great concern to most people. When I teach a seminar, the subject of relationships always surfaces because relationships are an important part of life and men and women are always looking for ways and means to make them work better.

Sometimes I ask the students in my class to raise their hands if any of them have been divorced, separated, married more than once or had difficulty in making a relationship work. Very slowly, people start to raise their hands, one by one, in a sheepish and embarrassed manner. I came to realize that nearly all people have problems with relationships because most don't understand what the ingredients are for a successful relationship.

There was one man who truly understood how relationships can be successfully implemented. This man was a great artist, poet and writer. He lived and died in Lebanon. Many years ago, I visited his home, I saw a gallery full of his pictures and I visited the stone sepulcher where he was buried on the side of a hill near the "Cedars of Lebanon." His name was Kahlil Gibran and of all the books he wrote, he considered *The Prophet* his greatest achievement. It was written at about the time of my birth in 1921. You may do yourself a great favor if you take the time to read in *The Prophet* the sections on marriage and friendship. Here Gilbran defines the great secret of a successful relationship with these words: "Love one another, but make not a bond of love. Let it rather be a moving sea between the shores of your souls."

He grasped and fully realized what love really is. Love is what you give out. In Chapter Two, I described how love is a male quality, an energy that goes in an outward direction. This male love energy is what both men and women can give to their partners. And this marvelous energy is what Gibran describes as "a moving sea between two souls." Your soul is the home of your spiritual body. Love moves like a stream from soul to soul. The words of the poet Rupert Brooke cast love as an immortal incandescence in whose fire we all but perish in delight:

> *"Oh! Love," they said "is King of Kings,*
> *And Triumph is his crown.*

Earth fades in flames before his wings,
And Sun and Moon bow down."

The poets, even the pragmatic scientists, and others, define love between man and woman as unifying and mysterious, but inspiring and as necessary as the breaths we breathe. The naturalist Loren Eisely has described love as the prime relationship between a man and a woman, as the singular motive that powers life itself and the creation of it by the Universal God. Whimsical as it may seem, Eisely, author of the *Immense Journey,* brilliantly relates the appearance of flowers on earth to the sudden start of humans on the path to civilization, and inevitably characterizes them as expressions of human love and sentiment:

"If one could run the story of that first human group like a speeded-up motion picture through a million years of time, one might see the the stone in the hand change to the flint ax and the torch. All that swarming grassland world with its giant bison and trumpeting mammoths would go down in ruin to feed the insatiable and growing numbers of a carnivore who, like the great cats before him, was taking his energy indirectly from the grass. Later he found fire and it altered the tough meats and drained their energy even faster into a stomach ill adapted for the ferocious turn man's habits had taken.

"His limbs grew longer, he strode more purposefully over the grass. The stolen energy that would take man across the continents would fail him at last. The great Ice Age herds were destined to vanish. When they did so, another hand like the hand that grasped the stone by the river long ago would pluck a handful of grass seed and hold it contemplatively.

"In that moment, the golden towers of man, his swarming millions, his turning wheels, the vast learning of his packed libraries, would glimmer dimly there in the ancestor of wheat, a few seeds held in a muddy hand. Without the gift of flowers and the infinite diversity of their fruits, man and bird, if they had continued to exist at all, would be today unrecognizable. Archaeopteryx, the lizard-bird, might still be snapping at beetles on a sequoia limb; man might still be a nocturnal insectivore gnawing a roach in the dark. The weight of a petal has changed the face of the world and made it ours."

And consider the genius of the Great Central Mind (God) whose powers were, and are, so vast that a plan of creation could define, in advance, the evolution of flowers whose presence foreshadowed the progress of man. When we contemplate the developing scheme of things in the changing world of our remote ancestors — apes becoming men because of the inscrutable wisdom of nature which endowed flowers with the new energy men would require of them to become human — it seems to me that the master mosaic of life was based on the enduring concept of love. It would be best characterized as the deep attraction between man and woman.

So, it seems the power of the relationship you may have with another person is based on a concept as old as the flowers that populate the earth, and probably more ancient still, as the key to life offered by God to his children.

Returning our thoughts to Gibran, he intimates that it is good to share the same home, your possessions and your life experiences with another, but not at the expense of your independence. He wrote, "Stand together yet not too close together. For the pillars of the temple stand apart."

This is correct. Two people in a relationship are similar to two separate pillars. Each of the couple is a pillar of strength to the other and standing apart helps to maintain the individual's independence.

One of the couple is the male pillar with all the powerful masculine energy of outgoing love. The other partner is the female pillar with the intuitive wisdom and understanding of a woman. Man and woman are supporting pillars of a temple which is "your home and your relationship."

Two people have different characteristics, but side by side they have the opportunity to complement each other. Gibran's final words on this subject of relationships remind us to "Let there be spaces in your togetherness." You must understand that the more opportunity and space you give your partner to become who he or she is bound to be, the more likely your relationship will be a success.

I asked a married friend of mine, who spends time away from home on business, "How do you both handle being separated for such long periods of time?"

He said, "We appreciate each other so much more when we come together again. It also gives us the opportunity to do things that we desire to do on our own."

In other words, "Absence makes the heart grow fonder." Allowing yourselves spaces in your togetherness is vital and important to a successful relationship. Relationships are usually thought of as involving two people. However, you can experience a relationship with yourself. The two elements of male and female can be found within yourself. That is why some people can live alone and be entirely happy and satisfied. They recognize the two aspects, male and female, of their being. They integrate these opposings and bring them into a state of oneness. They create for themselves a balanced life of intuitively knowing what to do and lovingly performing their accomplishments in service. Their male and female energies are like two currents moving between the shores of the ocean of life. The golden key to relationships is love, whether it be in loving yourself or another person.

Love is powerful, it purifies and cleanses any difficulties that may exist in your relationship. It sweeps away barriers that need to be removed. Love is like a divine lubrication that keeps the wheels of life turning within your relationship. Love, in that sense, is not life itself, but is the power that makes it possible for you to live happily with your partner. Love is a motion that is always moving outward, away from yourself toward the other person in your relationship. The meaning of love was expressed grandly by Swinburne when he wrote:

Ask nothing more of me, sweet,
All I can give you I give;
Heart of my heart, were it more
more would be laid at your feet:
Love, that should help you live,
Song that should spur you to soar.

Swinburne's lines bring me to the next point. Love is a giving process; you can never really receive love. This statement may confuse you because you may not fully understand the nature of love. The truth of the matter is that when you give love, you feel a glow; it makes you feel good. It is not what you receive from others that makes you feel good, but what you give to others. If you want to be happy and enjoy life, you should always be giving out love in some form or another. It is more blessed to give than to receive.

There is one particular matter that I always discuss with students when I teach a seminar, and discuss relationships. Many come for the wrong reasons. They pay their money with the hopes of buying the information to get a better relationship, make more money, have better health, or whatever they think they need in life.

I explain how my function as a teacher is to tell them exactly the opposite. I tell them that I will show them how they can give of their talents, make their abilities available, share their skills and bestow their love on others. I point out that for them to succeed, they need to develop the giving process so they will be able to receive and prosper. "Givers gain and takers lose," I tell them. This is certainly true of any sound relationship, because if you truly love someone else, all you want to do is to give this other person love. You are unconcerned whether or not love is given to you. If you are worried about how much you are going to get, then your marriage or relationship is unlikely to last very long.

Many people never really get married in the first place. All they do is to make a business agreement with their partner. They say, "If you love me, then I will love you. However, if you quit loving me, then I will seek a divorce." Love doesn't work that way. If you really love another person, it is unimportant whether you receive love back, because you know the great secret of loving, which was expressed by Conrad Aiken when he wrote:

Music I heard with you was more than music,
And bread I broke with you was more than bread.

The power of love, when sincere, can fill any void and is invincible.

I have a marriage or relationship test that you may like to try out for yourself. First of all, sit with your partner on a long couch, say about eight feet in length. You sit at one end with your partner at the other end. Next, both of you sit on your hands, shut your eyes, close your mouths and keep them closed so that you cannot talk to each other. Now, if you are perfectly happy and content sitting a few feet apart without any physical contact, with no talking and unable to

see each other, you are very blessed. You have a loving relationship which will last a long, long time. If you have to
open your eyes and peek at your partner or touch him with
your hand, then you may need to reexamine your relationship. While this test is far from foolproof, it may indicate
the need to reaffirm your feelings. Certainly, there is
nothing wrong with a physical relationship. It can be very
satisfying and beautiful, but you may require more than that
to keep a marriage working. You need to have an emotional
feeling for each other, to connect mentally and most
important of all, you need to be one with each other at the
spiritual level. In other words, you have to be married at all
four levels; physical, emotional, mental and spiritual. When
connections are made at all of the four body levels, then
your relationship will last forever. These four body levels
are described in Chapter Four. Physical and emotional
contact is easily accomplished. Mental connection is often
overlooked. You should have similar interests, like reading,
going to movies, watching television, political views or
listening to music. Spiritual contact is of the highest
priority. Sharing the same values and standards is
important. Share the same beliefs and preferably be active
in the same church and religion. When you are each one
with God, you will automatically be one with each other,
both linked to the same source. Connect in as many ways as
you possibly can to enjoy a relationship of oneness forever
and ever.

It was Rainer Maria Rilke who captured so briefly and
engagingly the ideas I've just expressed:

"A good marriage is that in which each appoints
the other guardian of his solitude."

Unfortunately, there are many people who seek only
to make physical contact with their partner. They are

attracted to the many glossy colored magazines like *Playboy* and *Playgirl* and others full of pictures of naked bodies. The implication is that if you seek out a good looking body and marry it, you will be the envy of your friends and you will live happily ever after. Not so, the body you marry deteriorates with age and after a while does not look so good. What do you do? Very simple, you get a divorce — rid yourself of this older and not-so-good-looking model and trade it for a new and better looking model. Such surface attachments seldom last..

In India, many years ago, a very beautiful way of life used to be practiced, which will help you understand the four levels of consciousness you possess but often do not heed. In India, however, the four levels represent periods of living.

First of all, as an Indian you would start off as a baby and slowly but surely develop physically into a full sized grown up. You would spend much time in your early years eating quantities of food and indulging in sports and games. This marks the *physical* growth period of your life. Second, as a young adult, you would enter the *emotional* period of your life. You would experience strong feelings, your hormones would start to function, and you would become sexually active.

As you mature, you are attracted to and seek out a partner for life. You marry and have children. You have beautiful feelings of love for your spouse and your children. In India, this is called the "householder stage of life" — the stage when you make your nest, have a home, raise children and display feelings of love to your whole family.

Third, when your eldest child is old enough to look after the family and whatever business you might have created, you the parent, might leave home to enter the *mental* period of life. In India, this is known as the "forest dwelling stage." You may literally go off into the forest to be alone and develop your mental capacity. You would practice centering, meditation, fasting, yoga and other disciplines you feel led to follow. Finally, when you have developed your mental abilities, you would return to the every day world and go back to the place where you were born and sit in the market place. There you would enter into the fourth state of consciousness, the *spiritual* stage. You might become a Guru or spiritual teacher. (When I am in India, I am often honored with the title of Guru because I teach spiritual matters.) You might even become a renunciate, a Swami or a Sadhu (a Holy Man). In other words, you might become a person to whom others could look for spiritual advice since you would have fully developed all of your four body levels — physical, emotional, mental and spiritual. The whole process is a very charming practice. However, in this day and age, hardly anyone in India follows this pattern. It is but a memory of a delightful practice from the past.

Nevertheless, these four stages do exist within you. When you were a small child, you depended a great deal on *physical* contact. You liked to be held, to clasp hands and to touch other people. Your relationships were very physical. Then, when you entered the *emotional* level as a young adult, your relationships between yourself and others were based largely on feelings. You didn't reason much, just reacted the way you did because you felt that way. Next, the *mental* level came into play, and your relationships became more thoughtful. You depended on your ability to think, to rationalize, to use the art of conversation. The final *spiritual* level was seldom experienced. That is why the concept of oneness wasn't and isn't experienced very much.

If you develop your spiritual consciousness, your relationship with another person will exceed your expectations. It was the fine novelist Willa Cather who wrote two observations that so aptly fit the idea of failure of growth of consciousness most of us practice:

Her first observation: "There are only two or three human stories, and they go on repeating themselves as fiercely as if they had never happened before."

This truism certainly reflects the general failure to explore our consciousness.

"Artistic growth [Cather wrote, and she may well have substituted the term 'spiritual' for 'artistic'] is, more than it is anything else, a refining of the sense of truthfulness. The stupid believe that to be truthful is easy; only the artist, the great artist, knows how difficult it is."

If you do connect inwardly with another person, you will discover an understanding that is beyond thinking, feeling and physical contact. You will find the eight-foot couch experiment most rewarding. Spiritual connection between two people is the highest form of relationship that can be experienced. This is the state of being in which both parties are so busy giving unconditional love to each other that they have no thought of looking for anything in return. They both realize that the giving of love is what makes them feel happy and fulfilled. This is where oneness is manifest; there is no separation between the couple because both are relating from their highest level of consciousness — their spiritual state of awareness.

Such a state of being approaches the glory of the union of two as I believe it has been perceived by the Universal Spirit. The understanding that results from such a relationship leads eventually to the profound discovery that every significant religion in the world has embraced: "Each person is," in the words of Mrs. Radha Burnier of the Theosophical Society of America, "the dispenser of his own glory or gloom: Each is his own lawgiver. This thought can be found in every religion in the world."

Mrs. Burnier added, that "If a [person] is to discover the Divine within, he cannot do it with his finite mind. He must transcend his personal self and his pride of separateness. He must work to find the hidden God within, worship him in the unholy, feed him in the hungry, love him in the unloving."

Of course, couples who practice what Mrs. Burnier believes become the kind of parents whose children grow up and develop the ability to have fulfilling relationships. When a child is born, it has just come from the mother's womb, it suckles on mother's breasts, has a very close relationship with the mother and is totally dependent on her for it's existence. Ideally, this bond between mother and child should be fostered for the first seven years of a child's life, encouraging the relationship to be purely maternal. From seven to fourteen years of age, the father needs to be in charge. The male influence teaches the growing child how to take care of himself and survive in the world. The child now fosters a relationship with the father; with the paternal influence, the child learns to stand on his own two feet and become an adult. At fourteen, a child is no longer a child, but is a young adult ready to make decisions in life. At fourteen, young people are fully developed. They are sexually capable of reproducing a child. Their full range of brain cells is now operative. Psychologically, they are old enough to stand on their own. They are capable of making decisions for themselves and they need the opportunity to be accepted as responsible people. Unfortunately, society too often treats teenagers as if they were immature, and of course, teenagers act out that which is expected of them: they behave in an immature manner.

On arriving in America from England, I started to notice when visiting homes that parents would tell their children to take out the garbage. I soon found that this was a common practice in the United States. So one day I challenged a parent and asked him if he was training his child to become a professional garbage collector. I suggested that this parent take out the garbage and give the child a sense of responsibility by allowing him to cook the breakfast and do the family grocery shopping. If you trust your child by giving him or her the opportunity to be responsible, he will not only not let you down, but will relate to you and other people more effectively. Too often we look down on children and try to control them. We should be nurturing them in a way that helps them to take their place in society and be able to develop ongoing relationships of a lasting manner.

Shortly after arriving in America, I lived in Fort Worth, Texas. I owned and operated a restaurant there. That summer, I had to fly back to England for a couple of weeks. Next door to me there lived a Jewish family with a fourteen-year-old son. I asked this young man, Ken, if he would look after the cash register in my restaurant while I was in England. I told him, "You don't have to look after the running of the restaurant, I have a trained cook who will do that, I just want you to be in charge of the money, operate the cash register, pay the bills, bank the money each day and keep the records and books in good order."

On my return from England, the books were in better shape than I had left them. Every penny was accounted for. This fourteen-year-old boy grew by leaps and bounds. His parents were amazed that I had given their son such respon-

sibility because they had never really given him the opportunity to act as a young adult. Any person's chance to
develop a healthy and fulfilling relationship with another
individual is largely due to whether that person's parents
had, in the first place, installed in him a sense of trust and
responsibility, allowing him, in time, to trust, respond to
and develop a relationship with other people. It is up to us
to help the next generation to have better and improved
relationships.

The symbol for your eleventh personal power to relate
to another person is the number eleven itself. The number
eleven consists of two upright pillars standing parallel to
one another. Each upright pillar represents one person. Thus
the two uprights represent two people, man and woman.
The number eleven symbolizes the relationship between
two individual souls. The two uprights are like the two
pillars of a temple as mentioned in *The Prophet* by Kahlil
Gibran. The two pillars stand side by side, separate, but act
as one in a relationship. Each of the two people has his own
personal strength, harmonizing with the other in a unified
relationship. The male entity has the capacity to be outgoing
by nature and the female has the ability to provide
substance, intuitive wisdom and knowledge.

It is interesting also that the number eleven has been
thought of as the "eleventh hour," a time when two
opposing parties who hold different viewpoints meet
together to form a peaceful relationship. This designation,
which usually is translated to mean that "time is running
out," has been applied to several historic occasions. The
most well known was the signing of the armistice at the
conclusion of World War I. The peace agreement was
concluded at the eleventh hour, on the eleventh day, of the
eleventh month — 11:00 a.m. on November 11, 1918.

Supposedly, this triple eleven was to set the stage to prevent another world war from ever happening again and to create a peaceful relationship among the former warring countries. The armistice did not last, but perhaps we are still at the eleventh hour, since so many people are anxious to bring peace to the world and create a relationship of oneness between all of us who live on planet Earth.

I well remember, as a child on Armistice Day in the 1930s, in England, that our school gathered with other schools around our local war memorial for two minutes of silence exactly at 11:00 a.m. on November 11th. Wearing Flanders poppies, we prayed for peace in the world. As children, we never thought that in a few short years, in 1939 to be exact, we would all be fighting again in World War II. To this day, I always remember on November 11, each year, the need for peaceful relationships between the nations of the world. I have never given up that one day there will be no more wars. The whole of my life's teachings are aimed at creating peaceful and lasting relationships throughout the world. I do this by presenting seminars in many countries, including England, Switzerland, Russia, Canada, the United States, Japan, Hong Kong, Singapore, Australia and New Zealand.

I sometimes ask students if they have had a separation or a divorce in their life and if so why they can't get along with one particular person of their own choosing out of all the millions of people who live in this world. How can they expect to have peace on earth if they can't live happily with one other person of their own choosing? This is a sobering thought. We need to learn how to have a satisfactory and peaceful relationship with one person; then, perhaps, we can work to straighten out the whole of the world.

All of us need to be alert to the one major barrier that prevents relationships from being successful. That is the quality of dominance many of us exercise indiscriminately. Dominance arises when a person accepts the idea that when he gives love to another person, he should take care of him or her to the extent that he imposes his will. Love can be an excuse to control, influence and dominate the one loved. In other words, dominance is substituted for love. The loved one is smothered by devotion.

If you have a tendency to act this way, to possess, it means that you are functioning from the two lower body levels — the physical and emotional. You want to physically possess the other and have an emotional experience your way. It is not until you act from the higher body levels, especially the spiritual, that you come to desire to give openly and let your partner have the freedom to choose the way he or she wishes to be. Make sure that your love never becomes possessive.

You can have relationships with the animal kingdom as well as the human kingdom. I breed many different types of exotic animals as a hobby. I have special types of relationships with these animals. There is a wallaby that waits for me every morning to be fed and will try to climb up my pants if I am not prompt in giving it a slice of bread. I had a very old miniature donkey that had lost most of her teeth, so she needed to be given a particular type of senior feed. There is a blind deer that requires special attention. Two golden retriever dogs live outside in a kennel and they take me for a daily walk around a small lake on my property. I have a Siamese cat that sleeps every night on my bed. He starts off on my pillow, and when I accept his presence he then goes to the bottom of the bed for the rest of the night. A group of Canada geese come up to my home in the winter and stay there until I feed them some grain. One female goose is so tame that when she nests, she lets me put my hand under her to count the eggs. All of these animals and others that I raise, have a special relationship with me. None of them can talk or even give me a hug, yet I feel their love when they rub against my legs or lick my face and hands. In their silence and with their eyes, they express their feelings of love. I also sense that they know what I do for them is my way of expressing and giving my love. I definitely have a relationship with my animals.

You can also love plants. Plants will respond to love and affection by flourishing and flowering more profusely. Remember the English couple in Findhorn, Scotland whose vegetables astounded the world by growing so big from the affection lavished on them? Have you heard of people who are said to have "a green thumb" and have a loving way of causing plant life to grow and thrive? All life — mineral, vegetable, animal and human — responds to love, especially when that love comes from the spiritual level with a sense of oneness. This is unconditional love. Your eleventh personal power to relate with another being, whether it be a plant, a living creature or a human soul, will create for you endless, satisfying and loving relationships. With practice, you will realize that you can be, and already are, one with all living entities. For starters, try to maintain a fulfilled relationship with just one other person! If you practice to make that relationship the glory of your spiritual self, then you will be able to comprehend the inspiration that gave Edna St. Vincent Millay the insight to catch immortality in her poem, *Renascence,* part of which is printed here:

The world stands out on either side
No wider than the heart is wide;
Above the world is stretched the sky, —
No higher than the soul is high.
The heart can push the sea and land
Farther away on either hand;
The soul can split the sky in two,
And let the face of God shine through.

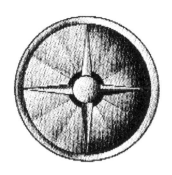

Chapter
Twelve

Longevity

When you cease to make a contribution, you begin to die.

Eleanor Roosevelt

This final chapter deals with the concept of human longevity, which I've come to view as a condition of the mind, a sort of cultural imperative, which has placed on us an unfair restriction on how long we can expect to live. But I've also come to the conclusion that our personal view of our individual life expectancy is irrevocably tied to the idea of significance — what we do to serve the world and make a statement of who we are in the process.

Our longevity, I believe, is absolutely related to how we view the world in which we live. Henry Margenau, the Eugene Higgins Professor of Physics and Natural Philosophy at Yale University, has aptly caught, in his views on significance, the confusion of our age, which certainly extends to the concept of aging:

"The problem of significance is not limited to our era nor to our station in the world; it springs from man's essential being and troubles him in all ages and wherever he exists. It is timeless, yet it has peculiar relevance to our times, whose confusion is characterized by loss of perspective and by misconceptions about the role of science in society and its threat to human values.

"Correct perspective can be gained only if we realize that events which we have ourselves experienced never seem as glorious or as dramatic as those conveyed to us in the songs of poets and through the eloquence of historians, who can afford to ignore the commonplace. The common impression that our age is undistinguished and decadent has therefore considerable psychological likelihood of being false. Consonant with this observation is the claim made by historians, the finding that every age has had its lamented maladies, and that the widely advertised gloom hovering over the present is hardly unique.

"On these grounds it is justifiable to dismiss, for example, the complaint that we have lost our spiritual values. In truth, these values are as evident as ever — perhaps even more evident in this day of public soul-searching over radio and television — but they are different; because we know more about the world, older values have lost their validity and their appeal, and our critical appraisal of previous standards is not only necessary but good.

"In a similar vein it is said that we are preoccupied with material things. If this means that we have more goods available for enjoyment, the statement is true, but it has no point because earlier civilizations were without them by necessity and not by choice; furthermore, let it be noted that we also have more churches and more poetry."

Now, to paraphrase Margenau, the problem of aging has a peculiar relevance to our times, because in a real sense it represents a deep misconception about the social status of older persons in our society as well as a confirmed idea we all share about how old we should be when we die.

As you will see, the whole concept of longevity ties into the pursuit of significance, as expressed by Margenau, and, fundamentally, to mysticism as it is expressed in "powers of the subtle body."

Some years ago, I was given a coffee mug on my sixty-fifth birthday. On it were inscribed the words, "Life Begins at 40." But a line was drawn through forty and, subsequently, through several ascending numbers: fifty, sixty. However, the number sixty-five was left intact. The message clearly was meant to convey that "Life Begins at 65."

More recently I have tried to find a mug with the imprint: "Life Begins at 70," or maybe even 75. But no such luck. It seems to be the opinion in our society that you should only live to a certain age and not go beyond. Now, I ask you, who sets these limits? The answer appears to be as I indicated earlier, that it is the system, our culture, that makes decisions for us. But the fact is, people live longer now than ever before. The reason for this, we are told, is because we have improved medical facilities and health care. Therefore it is okay now to live to about seventy years of age. There are the few who live to an older age like eighty, ninety, or even one hundred years of age, but they are the exception rather than the rule. Some don't even make it to seventy. However, the average age at death appears to be a little over seventy.

If we were to require more proof of the cultural emphasis on retirement at sixty-five, we only need to recognize that all large businesses and corporations are geared to let you go in your early sixties. Supposedly, you are too old to be effective, so you are put out to pasture to play golf, watch television, and possibly have some fun in the sun, like playing shuffleboard. Retirement funds, pensions, and Social Security are all geared to pay off at about the time you reach sixty-five. The actuaries, the men who calculate the risks and set the premiums for insurance companies, annuities, and pension funds, work on the basis that you will not live for more than an average of five years after you retire. It is a sobering thought to realize that everything is calculated around these figures. We human beings, being gregarious types, love to conform to the group consciousness. We wouldn't want to live too long and upset the insurance companies! You would probably feel guilty if you lived to be over a hundred. After all you always want to be like everybody else, don't you! You wouldn't want to rock the boat; that wouldn't be nice!

But the fact is that there are hundreds of examples of people who have learned how to grow older than the actuaries predict, and, with a younger body.

To verify the statement I've just made, I am going to call on Michael Murphy and Rhea White, authors of the book, *In the Zone*. In a section in which they describe extraordinary powers available to us humans, they refer to the Sanskrit word *siddhi* , *a* technical term deriving from Hindu spiritual practice. This word is often translated as "power" and "perfection." I should explain that *siddhi* refers not only to what we would call "occult" or "transcendent" powers, but also those of cognition of fundamental aspects of *true reality*.

Now, with full credit to the authors of *In the Zone,*
they created in their book a table in which they described
several specific powers deriving from the exercise of *siddhi.*
Then, across the printed page under the heading
"Accomplishments in Sport" they described the phenomena
of physical transformation or bodily change emanating
from the application of *siddhi.*

Since *In the Zone* mainly addresses extraordinary
psychic happening in sports, it is only natural that the
authors would have chosen reliable examples of *siddhi*
applications in a sports world frame of reference. Only two
examples from the table need to be examined here to prove
how the *siddhi* can cause bodily changes:

SIDDHI	ACCOMPLISHMENTS IN SPORT
• Exceptional control of bodily processes, feelings, thoughts, imagination, and other mental functions	Pulse, heartbeat, breathing and other physiological processes come under extraordinary control when a runner does the marathon in a little over two hours (which means an average of better than a mile every five minutes for the entire 26 miles), or when underwater swimmers hold their breath for more than five minutes at depths of up to forty feet, or when a race driver makes the hairpin turns required in Grand Prix driving.
• Mastery of pain, both psychic and physical	Football players have gone through games with broken ribs, noses, toes, and fingers. Boxers have finished fights with broken hands and wrists. Often there is no pain at all during the contest, so great is the player's concentration.

In their table, the authors listed under *siddhi* that which is the subject of our own inquiry: "Freedom from the aging process." Under Accomplishments in Sport was the following:

"George Blanda, at 45, was starring for the Oakland Raiders. Sam Snead was a money winner on the PGA tour at age 65. Percy Cerutty, the famous track coach, was a physical dynamo until the day he died. Bernard McFadden parachuted into the Seine and the Thames on his 85th and 86th birthdays. Track and swimming records for people over 40 are falling at a rapid rate."

I should add that in the higher states of spiritual attainment, the body becomes ever-born, ever-renewed and self-existent. In other words: aging without meaning or relationship to temporal measurements.

Authors Murphy and White make a provocative statement in a chapter following the one in which they introduced the power of *siddhi:*

"Given the similarities between sport and religious practice, the question arises whether sportspeople can deliberately promote metanormal functioning. Could the kind of experience we have described in the preceding chapters be systematically developed? Part of the answer is clear: Coaches and athletes in many parts of the world are already using methods from yoga, the martial arts, hypnosis, meditation, and other disciplines to enrich their training programs. During the 1960s, a field of applied psychology called *psychic self-regulation* was developed in the Soviet Union. It is based on laboratory studies of our ability to control physiological processes, including pulse, muscular relaxation, blood pressure, and breathing."

The question I now propose is this: If there are spiritual processes (siddhi) by which we can delay or stop aging, as sports figures described by Murphy and White in their book have, what's preventing us from slowing or delaying or stopping the aging process? What is stopping us from systematically developing the kinds of spectacular experiences that seem to defy the imagination?

Why can't we stop the clock?

Strange as it may seem, a major part of the answer lies in the antagonism of many formal religions for the study, application and concept of spirituality as narrowly inter preted by them.

Brian Luke Seaward, in his marvelous book, *Stand Like Mountain, Flow Like Water, Reflection on Stress and Human Spirituality,* addresses this problem with great clarity and kindness. I am reproducing his remarkable statement here with his permission:

"Several years ago, I heard a symphony conductor interviewed on National Public Radio. In his attempt to express the essence of classical compositions, he said music was a universal language that could be understood at some level by everyone.

"'Music,' he said, 'has a very spiritual essence. When we listen to music, we eavesdrop on the thoughts of God.' What he said next really grabbed my attention. 'We must distinguish the difference between spirituality and religion. Spirituality unites, where religions divide and separate.'

"When you hear the truth you feel it in your gut; it vibrates in every cell of your body. Upon hearing his words, I got goose bumps at the recognition of this wisdom.

"Sometimes defining what a concept is not becomes an explanation in itself. For instance, human spirituality is neither a religion nor the practice of a religion. Each religion is based upon a specific dogma: a living application of a specific set of organized rules based on the ideology of the human spirit. It is generally agreed that being actively involved in a particular religion is a way to enhance one's spirituality — to bring one closer to God. This is the primary objective of all religions. On the whole they are effective. But recently several experts in the field of humanistic psychology have noted that religion can often stifle the growth of the human spirit.

"This fact has led some behavioral psychologists to observe that people can form an addiction to a religion as a means of validating one's existence. By the same token, the practice of extreme rituals, such as prolonged sessions of meditation, are considered unhealthy if they eclipse other essential aspects of one's life. Religion can certainly promote spiritual evolution; the two are very compatible. Yet individuals can be very spiritual and not religious, just a people can be religious but have a poor awareness of their own spirituality.

"I have a clergy friend who states it this way: 'God has many the Church has not, and the Church has many God has not.'

"Recently a workshop participant shared with me a similar perspective, one that I'm sure came from her personal experience. She explained, 'Religion is for those who are trying to avoid hell; spirituality is for those who have been there.'

"I describe spirituality as water that flows freely everywhere. Water, like spirit, may take on different shapes but it is found everywhere. Religions are like containers that hold water; they come in all shapes and sizes. But water doesn't need a container to exist. To understand the concept of spirituality you have to experience it; rarely will two interpretations be the same. Although spirituality and religion are separate but related concepts, it is impossible to separate the concept of spirituality from the divine aspect of the universe.

"The poet Maya Angelou says, 'I cannot separate what I conceive as Spirit from my concept of God. Thus I believe that God is Spirit.'

"This is the most exciting time to be alive. At no other point in our history has so much information become accessible to so many people. We have an unprecedented freedom to assimilate the great wisdom from around the world. By comparison, centuries ago the vast majority of the world's population could not read. Information was spoon-fed and the control over what information was released was immense. Now, as pieces of the cosmic puzzle become assembled from all cultures, religions and societies — specifically those pieces that highlight various aspects of ageless wisdom — we begin to see that there are common denominators that bind the human spirit. Spirituality unites, whereas religions divide and separate.

"In this time of humanity, it is a time to unite.

"In the words of Christian theologian Matthew Fox, 'We are living in a post-denomination age.' Bearing this in mind, it becomes imperative that we learn to set aside our cultural, religious and political differences and work together as one people. Today, the world is experiencing many wake-up calls in an effort to raise consciousness. The answers to global problems will not come from separateness, but from unity."

What I have written about age stopping or slowing has been put forth to emphasize what we are capable of, but few of us ever do. Learning is a slow process, and we make progress slowly.

In the meantime, as you begin to form strong ideas about your spiritual capabilities, you may be interested in some of the things I have discovered to stay young and to acquire a longer life on earth. First, I have set my age goal as 120 years. You may say, why not, if the doctors say that is possible.

Here is the reason I believe it will happen: because I accept that it is okay to live to 120. I have read numerous books on the subject of longevity and many mention the concept of living six score years. This information reinforces my feeling that it can be done. In order to make sure that my mind would accept the concept of living to 120, I did something very special. Some years ago I held my sixtieth birthday party. I printed out formal invitations to all my friends on which was written the following words: "Come and celebrate with Alexander and his friends the halfway mark in his life to become 120!" And the interesting thing is that when I checked out the guest register I found that 120 people had come to my sixtieth birthday party. I still show a copy of this invitation to people to this day. Why? Because every time I think about it, talk about it, and share this incident in my personal life with people like you, it reinforces my mind that I am actually going to live that long.

The symbol for this law number twelve is based on the number twelve. Throughout history we have always measured time in divisions of twelve. The sun, which is the center of the solar system, moves in a large circle every 25,000 years and this period of time is divided into twelve equal divisions commonly known as the twelve signs of the zodiac. When you divide 25,000 by twelve, you end up with twelve periods of approximately 2,100 years. You also know that each year is divided into twelve months. Also there are twelve hours A.M., before noon and twelve hours P.M., after noon. Twelve is the number for measuring time. The ancients used the zodiac as the symbol for measuring time and longevity, whereas modern man tends to use the clock face with its twelve hours as the symbol for living to a great age. Father Time and the hourglass are also associated with the concept of time and longevity. Perhaps you can now see why I have always been attracted to the idea of living to 120, because quite simply all you have to do is to add a zero to the number twelve which represents the law of longevity.

One reason I have chosen to live to 120 is that I have always been interested in the stories concerning Moses in the Bible. Moses is said to have lived 120 years. He spent the first forty years of his life in Egypt in the courts of Pharaoh, learning all the knowledge of that day and age. From forty to eighty years of age he fed the flocks of Jethro, meditating and growing spiritually. When he was eighty, God spoke to him from the burning bush. He was given instruction by God and led the Israelites out of Egypt to the Promised Land. The journey lasted forty years, and he died at 120 years of age when his mission was complete. During the first forty years of my life, I was an educator and taught school and grew intellectually. When I became forty, I started to study deeper issues and picked the direction of spiritual growth. I am still doing that. However, when I am eighty, I feel I will be sufficiently prepared to help people on a modern day journey to a peaceful world here on planet Earth. That is my dream, my mission as it has come to me. It is my personal significance.

Of course, there are practical aspects that must be acknowledged if you are to prepare yourself for an advanced age. Among them is the realization that you must look after your body so that it will remain healthy, active and supportive of your desire for long life. For most people, it is not until they make the decision to live longer that they pay attention to their physical body needs. That was certainly true for me. I have always been conscious of right eating all my life, but it was not until I was forty that I considered an exercise program.

I have already shared with you the most important thing to do, which is to set your goal of living to a specific age. Then continue to focus this goal until you fix it on your brain cells, until you focus out into your life the results you desire. The more you talk about it and think about it, the deeper the impression becomes on your brain, so that your physical body will conform to the age image you have selected. As you know, whatever your mind conceives, your body will achieve. However, the brain-body relationship, as great as it is, can always use some practical assistance, such as proper nutrition and exercise.

The value of proper nutrition became much clearer to me when I read John Robbins's *Diet for a New America.* After reading what Robbins wrote, I centered myself and listened for inner guidance from my intuition. First of all, I was directed toward health products and, shortly afterward, I became aware of *Matol* from Montreal, Canada. I started to drink *K.M.,* a potassium and mineral supplement twice daily. *K.M.* is a liquid that purifies and oxidizes the blood and removes toxins. Every morning, I ate a bowl of their breakfast cereal as well as consuming a couple of food bars each day. These products were of a high quality and I consumed them on a regular basis for about two to three years.

Next I came across a book, *The Cure for all Cancers,* by Hulda Regeher Clark in which I discovered a program laid out step by step on how to purge the body of parasites which are considered to be the cause of many diseases, especially cancer. I followed this program for exactly one year to make sure that I rid my body of parasites and flushed out metals and toxins to keep myself healthy through the use of the following herbs: black walnut hulls from the black walnut tree; wormwood from the artemisia tree; common clove from the clove tree.

Next came *Essiac Tea,* manufactured by Flora Inc., and made famous by a nurse, Rene Caisse, who received the recipe from an old Indian medicine man of the Ojibwa Indian tribe from Ontario, Canada. Many cures of various forms of cancer have been credited through the use of *Essiac Tea.* (Essiac is Caisse spelled backwards.)

Shortly afterward, I discovered another company from Canada in Vancouver, British Columbia called Two Touch, which has created a product called *Radical Force.* This capsule product contains the same four ingredients that are found in *Essiac Tea,* namely burdock root, sheep sorrel, slippery elm bark and rhubarb root, with the addition of spirulina. *Radical Force* enhances the body's natural ability to ward of sickness and fight disease. Another product, *Radical Sweep,* detoxifies the blood and acts as a body cleanser.

Articles on the power of *Pycnogenol* directed me to the history of the French explorer, Jacques Cartier, who discovered Canada's Gulf of St. Lawrence in 1534. His crew became sick trying to survive on salted meat and biscuits. A Quebec Indian showed the sailors how to brew a tea based on the bark of a pine tree. The crew recovered and today, more than four hundred years later, *Pycnogenol,* a powerful all-natural antioxidant that supports our natural ability to fight free radicals, is sold by Kaire International.

A friend of mine introduced me to the macrobiotic diet based on eating three simple meals a day. The main foods to be consumed are organic short-grain brown rice, sea vegetables, beans and lots of green vegetables (such as broccoli), oatmeal cookies and twig tea. This rigorous process is not easy to follow, because you have to cook at home and can't eat out in restaurants. However, for those who do follow the macrobiotic diet, they lead healthy disease-free lives. In spite of its benefits, the macrobiotic way of life, I felt, was not for me.

Finally, I became aware of aromatherapy. Aromatherapy is an ancient knowledge that goes back to the Egyptians and is mentioned in the Bible, both in the Old and New Testament, numerous times. It deals with the essential oils, which are the blood and heartbeat of the plant kingdom. The health giving properties of these living essential oils are antioxidant, antiviral and antibacterial and have anti-infectious properties as well as providing immune stimulus for the body. These natural oils are truly a gift from God. I have found out that there is only one company in the world that produces high quality oils that are pure, unadulterated and not diluted. This company produces one hundred different individual and blended oils as well as a long line of food supplements, including mineral essences and vitamins, that are all mixed with essential oils. Oils can be diffused into the air as a fine mist to be breathed into the body or placed on the body itself and used in connection with massage. I can't say enough in the praise of aromatherapy and how it strengthens my immune system and keeps me healthy. As far as I am personally concerned, I have found what is right for Alexander. For further information regarding any of the above products, please write to me at the address at the back of this book.

I have described a few of the health-producing foods, herbs and plants that can augment your health. I suggest searching on your own for other natural products to increase your health. I suggest that you follow your hunches and listen to your own inner voice and decide what route you wish to follow. We are all unique and are attracted to different methods to keep our bodies healthy, so that longevity can become a reality for us. Why not join the 120 club!

To make the end of this chapter, I thought a long while to write something that would stick in the the reader's mind. Finally, I decided to call once more upon Brian Luke Seaward, author of *Stand Like Mountain, Flow Like Water,* who is a renowned speaker on spirituality, who in a few lines of marvelous prose, has summed up the message of this book:

> Stand Like Mountain
> Flow Like Water

> To walk the human path is hard,
> To stay put is not an option.
> At times my head is filled with doubt,
> I pause, uncertain and insecure,
> Then I hear these words aloud,
> *Stand like mountain, flow like water.*

> I walk each step in search of truth,
> My quest brings both joy and sorrow.
> Light and dark dance unified Yes!
> Balance is the key to life.
> Again I hear the words aloud,
> *Stand like mountain, flow like water.*

> We come to Earth to learn to love,
> A lesson we all must master.
> To know and serve the will of God,
> Is not a task for a chosen few.
> We must each answer the call to love,
> *Stand like mountain, flow like water.*

Let Love move through your Life to be Light to the world.

Blessings upon blessings

Alexander Everett

Appendix
A

World Service — A Way of Life!

Outline	Physical	Emotional	Mental	Spiritual
Part One:	Right Eating	Love Myself	Be Positive	Develop My
I Serve	Proper Exercise	Be Open to	Set Goals	Intuition by
Myself	Be with Nature	Receiving	Create Wealth	Centering
Part Two:	Give of Myself	Show Love,	Perceive and	Be an Example
I Serve	Take Time Out	Compassion	Image Oneness	Be My Own
Others	Do Good Deeds	and Devotion	of all People	Divine Self
Part Three:	Recycle:	Reduce:	Read How to	Show Respect
I Serve	Glass, Metal,	Electricity,	Help the	I Won't Litter
The Earth	Paper, Plastic	Fuel and Water	Environment	or Pollute

Part One: How I Serve Myself

Physically — I work on my body by keeping it in a healthy and fit condition. If I am not already a vegetarian I need to go more in that direction. I cut back on meat consumption until I eliminate all animal products from my diet. Suitable exercise such as aerobics is essential to keep my muscles and limbs properly stretched so as to permit a flow of oxygen in my bloodstream. I need to set aside twenty to thirty minutes per day for fast walking, jogging, jumping rope, cycling, running or rowing. Also, I must spend as much time as possible in the peace and quiet of nature.

Emotionally — I need to accept who I am by loving myself more and to be open to receive as well as to give.

Mentally — I must develop constructive thinking. Use affirmation if need be. Check out and pay attention to what I read and watch on television. Set goals that will create wealth and fulfill my daily needs. I remember that my life works in direct proportion to the goals that I set and the commitments that I make and keep.

Spiritually — I center myself every day early in the morning. I do this to awaken my intuition, so that I may receive guidance and find the answers that I need to keep myself physically fit, emotionally stable and mentally sound.

Part Two: How I Serve Others

Physically — I will set aside time to be with other people on a one-on-one basis and use my gifts and talents to help others to become more effective. Perform good deeds large and small. Join an organization that touches my heart, in the community where I live, such as handicapped children, the illiterate, the blind, those with AIDS, the elderly, shut-ins, Meals on Wheels, etc. Serve on a regular basis one day a month or so many hours per week. I will only commit myself to what is realistic for me.

Emotionally — I will serve with compassion, love and devotion. I remember that the quality of service is more important than the length of time I serve, because one sincere small service performed for another human being can change that life forever.

Mentally — I constantly perceive and image oneness between all people. I see the Divinity in everybody. I serve with the understanding that the server is one with the person being served. I eliminate all thinking of separation. I know my life will improve in direct proportion to how much I give of my time to others.

Spiritually — I will help people in the way that I am inwardly led to do. I must be my own Divine Self and let that Divinity shine through me so that I may be a light to the world.

Part Three: How I Serve the Earth

Physically — I recycle newspapers, brown paper sacks, glass bottles, all kinds of metals and plastic material. I save everything I possible can, because with the rapid increase of the population, I realize the world may run out of natural resources.

Emotionally —I make the decision to consume less. I reduce the amount of electricity I use. I turn off the lights at night. I drive a car that burns less gas. I use water sparingly. I fix the faucets that drip. I eat less or no meat at all. It takes sixteen pounds of grain to produce one pound of beef. I realize that if we all became vegetarians and ate the grains directly, starvation would be erased from the face of the earth. I must live simply, so that the rest of the world may simply live.

Mentally — I read books on how to help the environment. I join an organization that fosters projects concerning ecology. I spread the word and get involved with World Service.

Spiritually — I remember that we are all one. I show respect. I don't litter and make life undesirable for other people or dangerous for the animals or harmful to plant life. I pick up garbage, helping to keep the environment pure and healthy. If I keep my body clean by eating natural foods, I am helping keep my home, the earth, spotless, unpolluted and healthy. I need to be aware of that!

Appendix
B

Centering Procedure

On this page and the following, is a more detailed version of the centering language that Alexander Everett uses to teach Inward Bound:

I Now Prepare to Center Myself

I close my eyes for peace and quiet.
I straighten my spine to stimulate energy flow.
I open my hands to receive,
And I just let go and R-E-L-A-X, R-E-L-A-X.
Whenever I hear the word "relax" mentioned
I let go more of my outer physical body,
My emotions and my mind so that
I may be more aware of my inner beingness.
I just let go and R-E-L-A-X, R-E-L-A-X.

I first visualize the color RED.
I relax my body from head to foot.
I relax — let go of my body — relax.
I next visualize the color ORANGE.
I release and let go my emotions.
I desire only that which is good for others.
I now move down the rainbow to YELLOW.
I calm and still my mind.
I bring my mind to rest.
The next color I visualize is GREEN.
I allow peace to come into my life.
I sense a state of peacefulness within.
I now move down the rainbow to BLUE.
I let love permeate my entire being.
I feel myself full of love.
I next bring into focus the color PURPLE.
I seek out the depths within.
I aspire to that inner, secret place.
I lastly visualize the color VIOLET.
I enter the innermost part of my being.
I am now there — I am centered.

PEACE — PEACE — PEACE

I am now one with my Inner Self,
A state that encompasses all of time.
So I just become aware of the totality of the Now.
I am only conscious of the present.
I feel and sense this one moment in time.
I just realize myself right now.
I feel and sense the center of my being.
I am at one with my Inner Self.
I am calm — I am still — I am at peace.

And as I become aware of my oneness with Peace,
I center myself in this indwelling presence of Peace.

PEACE — PEACE — PEACE

To help me remain centered and to be at peace,
I place myself in my scene from nature.
I use all my five senses to let this come to pass.
I see the wonders of creation that surround me.
I hear the sounds of nature loud and clear.
I smell the fragrance that permeates the air.
I taste of the great beauty that fills my scene.
I am touched by the very movement of nature.
This oneness with all life draws me ever inward
And I become more centered than ever before.

PEACE — PEACE — PEACE

For the next few minutes I will remain centered
with my eyes closed and I will experience
whatever I am led to experience.

PEACE — PEACE — PEACE

I NOW PREPARE
TO RETURN TO THE EVERYDAY WORLD.

I come back slowly from the center of my being,
from the inner to the outer.

I remember that, after centering myself,
Spiritually, I am more enlightened;
Mentally, I am more enriched with pure thoughts;

Emotionally, I am enthused with love for others;
Physically, I am energized with the fullness of life.

And whatever the spirit leads me to do
I now know that I can do this better than ever before.
For after centering myself, I find that
With this inner spiritual power available to me,
All things are possible in my life and this is so.

Now in a few moments I need to open my eyes.
So I prepare to visualize the colors of the rainbow
in reverse sequence — starting with —
    The innermost color,   VIOLET,
    Moving up and out to   PURPLE,
    Then further up to   BLUE,
    Then to   GREEN,
    Next,   YELLOW,
                      ORANGE,
                        RED.

I open my eyes and I am wide awake.
I am enlightened, enriched, enthused and energized.

                I JUST AM.

Ordering Information

Centering Tape as discussed in Chapter Ten.
Side One: Short Version (15 minutes)
Side Two: Long Version (30 minutes)
Price $12 includes shipping and handling.

Genius Within (six cassette tapes each one hour long)
Alexander helps you to discover the genius within you and
how to use it.
Price $55 includes shipping and handling.

Inner Wealth (six cassette tapes each one hour long)
Alexander shows you how to master the laws of life.
Some of this material is in this book.
Price $55 includes shipping and handling.

 To obtain any of the above cassette tapes or
information regarding health products, especially
AROMATHERAPY as mentioned in Chapter Twelve, please
write to:

Alexander Everett
P. O. Box 456
Veneta, Oregon 97487
or
Phone: 541-683-2121

To order additional copies of

Inward Bound

Book: $15.00   Shipping/Handling $3.50

Contact: ***BookPartners, Inc.***
P.O. Box 922, Wilsonville, OR 97070
Fax: 503-682-8684
Phone 503-682-9821
Phone: 1-800-895-7323